*If "seeking first to understand" is a habit for effectiveness, Ruby's work is multi-purpose. While many bemoan the status quo or seem overwhelmed, her work offers viable solutions and challenges our thinking. The model provides insights about our perceptions and pushes our "buttons." We have found that Ruby's work—as a catalyst for open dialogue—resonates with community leaders from all sectors, including education, business, human services, and the faith community. It skillfully offers **practical strategies for members of all economic classes to build social capital and human capacity**—for ourselves and our communities. Ruby's work has become an integral part of our work.*

—Dr. Jan Young, Executive Director
Assisi Foundation of Memphis, Inc., Memphis, TN

What this work does in the school improvement area is bring in the support that people really need. I've watched schools go from 5% of their eighth-grade mathematics students passing the state assessment to 60% of their students passing. That's what people want, and that's what this work does.

*I've had a lot of experience using the school improvement process both as an outside consultant and within a district in which I've worked. And I can say without a doubt that **every school I've worked with has improved no less than 20% within the first year.** That's amazing to me, and in the school district where I recently worked the high school-level science exit scores have gone from 60% passing to 87% passing, which is phenomenal. What does that mean? That means kids have a choice about what they do in life. They can't graduate from high school if that haven't passed that exit-level assessment. So when they're passing that assessment they have a choice about what they'll be doing with their future.*

—Shelley Rex, Director of Elementary Humanities
for Spring Independent School District, Spring, TX
aha! Process Math Consultant

The first year that we implemented the aha! process using A Framework for Understanding Poverty, **we saw a 23% increase in academic achievement using the principles** *from the process.*

This training empowered me as an administrator. I've been able to communicate the vision of the aha! process and the framework of understanding poverty. It fits with the person that I am so it has resonated far beyond me to my fellow administrators, to my team, as well as to school leaders who are around me. We all see the vision and the value of using the aha! process—what it can do for students, as well as for individual teachers.

—Kenneth Fleming, Principal
Glendale Elementary School District, Grades 4–8,
Glendale, AZ

I would say out of the 12 tests we gave, 11 were at least 20 points up—to 60 or 70 points higher than the national norm. So yes, I think a lot of this does make an improvement. But I think it's a team effort with the teachers, the students, the administration and hopefully our high expectations for knowing all students can do it.

I would say probably **75–80% of the student body moved up what we call a quadrant.** *A quadrant is starting from red up to blue and we had probably 75–85% move from red, which is below proficiency to blue, which is advanced, and there are four quadrants. So yes, I'd say about 75% of our students are moving.*

—Maureen di Stasio, Middle School Principal
Widefield School District No. 3, Colorado Springs, CO

It is **phenomenal the way it has improved our building, specifically, but all of the consortium schools.** *It makes a difference for an individual teacher, but it can also transform a building. It is a different way of thinking, which influences your planning and influences the data that you will acquire and then use for that planning.*

—Margaret O'Connor-Campbell
Campus Director at Archdiocese of Indianapolis, IN

We had been into this process of implementing these processes and strategies for about three years [in Huntsville, TX]. And our 100th anniversary was a big year for us. **We received 21 gold achievement awards from the Texas Education Agency that year, and those are given for either increases in student achievement or increases in students' performance at the commended level**—*not just those who pass the exam but those who score in the A+ range, for example.*

In third-grade math we had a 65% increase in students performing at the commended level. In fourth-grade math a 54% increase. Fifth-grade math a 153% increase. Sixth-grade math a 73% increase. Seventh-grade math a 90% increase. Eighth-grade math a 180% increase. Eighth-grade science a 33% increase. And the exit-level high school science—I'm not kidding—a 2500% increase in students scoring at the commended level. Now that was in 2007–08. That was our record-breaking year. We **broke 13 records** *the next year, and we broke them again the next year. I'm very proud of those achievements.*

—Dr. Richard Montgomery, Superintendent
Star City School District, Star City, AR, and
Former Superintendent of Schools, Huntsville
Independent School District, Huntsville, TX

I think true educators want to continue their learning, and when they find ways where they can work together, where they can collaborate and it benefits kids, and where they can see the payoff for it, that does nothing but inspire you and motivate you to work a little harder. And I think that that's one of the things this work does.

What I like about Ruby's work is she always tries to **make it easier for teachers to use than not.** *Teachers don't have a lot of extra time, so we've got to have strategies that are high impact that are going to give us a high payoff. And the strategies in the 9 processes … I always say to people that they're not rocket science, but you get your payoff through your collaboration. You get your payoff through the consistency through which you implement them. You get your payoff over time when you keep refining those processes.*

—Dr. Donna Magee, Vice President of
Educational Services
aha! Process, Highlands, TX

If you're a principal and you're looking for something to change the morale, to improve student achievement, and to improve student discipline in your school, then use the framework process because we were successful with it. I continue to use it with my faculty, and it's worked for us.

We use the 15 behaviors of mutual respect; teachers bought into that and had an understanding and implemented that with the students. It changed students' attitudes, and it helped them become more focused and understand their own behavior, as well as what they were trying to accomplish in the classroom.

What we did was we looked at each student's state test scores, and then we grouped them by the ones who did not meet standards, the ones who met standards, and the ones who exceeded standards. And we really, really tried with the framework to move the students who did not meet the state standards into at least meeting standards, and we were very successful with it. **By using this, our scores in math and reading were always in the 90th percentile.**

—Lura Reed, Principal
Muscogee County School District, Columbus, GA

I use mental models through my teaching and everyday subjects I do in my classroom. This is a way for students to have some kind of mental picture in their head of how we use some things, and students are able to make some real-life connections.

I always tell my students that it doesn't matter where you live or your background or what you don't have or have, that they have what it takes, and it's just to do what they can. And I always tell my students that they have a brain, and that's all they need to be successful, and I always share my personal experience with them as well. And I make that connection with them, and I always ask them to tell me what they're going to do when they grow up. I ask them to come and see me when they become a professional in whatever they choose to be because I want them to know that I believe in them—and I think that that's where the success is for them too. **And I also think that's what has made us exemplary.**

—Rosie Flores, Teacher
Pearland Elementary School, Pearland, TX

I think I'm a good teacher [after attending all the trainings]. I think my kids are more successful, and I think my teachers are more successful because I can embed all those strategies in there. And it's become so second nature that I can look at a task now and tell you what input processes are needed to do that and what strategies I need to embed in order for the kids who don't have those automatically to be able to do them.

*One year my fourth-grade team came for a grade-level meeting, and they brought their benchmark assessments for math—and the kids had missed translations, reflections, and rotations, and they were also missing scanning in on their Scantron (they were having the right answer in the booklet but were coloring in the wrong bubbles on their Scantrons)—and I said, Well, that's because it's input processes—they're missing identifying data in space. So when **we started intentionally implementing those strategies to help the kids acquire that, then we started seeing huge, huge differences in mathematics and huge differences indirectly in language arts** because they were able to track better.*

—Karen Jensen
District Instructional Specialist, Killeen Independent
School District, Killeen, TX

*In Oklahoma we have an AYP score of 0–1500, and my school, which is large (60% Hispanic, 100% free and reduced lunches) "shouldn't" be performing as well as it does. Our AYP is usually around 1100–1200. **Our ELL students, which are 60% of our population, are scoring just as well as any other learners,** and we take that to mean we're being successful with all the methods that we have.*

—Judy Feary, Principal
Tulsa Public Schools, Tulsa, OK

When we academic coaches come in with the 9 processes [School Improvement] into a school, the first thing that I notice is that the teachers stop and understand the data. They see that Johnny counts more than one time. They become more interested in one student or two students who are in their class because they realize that could be the one who keeps their percentages down or puts them on school improvement or keeps them from being recognized—or whatever the gauge is in that state. When we know who to work with, then it makes our job so much easier. **Then we build that relationship, never give up, and the success stories happen.**

Ruby Payne's work benefits the veteran teacher in that no child is left out because we recognize every child and where every child is in the testing scheme. We now realize how many times they count, we understand which standards or which objectives they're not strong in, and every child is now identified. It benefits the brand-new teachers in that it gives them the test background to be able to have their students be successful.

—Sally Black, Math Teacher, Advanced Placement AB
and BC Calculus, Geometry
Goose Creek Memorial High School, Baytown, TX
aha! Process Math Consultant

It is transformative. I believe strongly in the work. I know personally—and with my 10 years of experience as a consultant—how it's changed teachers and staff to include custodial all the way through to administrative. For students, it's a case of making minor changes in some cases, to have an enormous impact on a student's life—to go from being shut off, isolated, not participating at all to engaged, inquisitive, inquiring, participating in a class and extending that beyond the class to where that student is now part of the community.

—Connie Abernathy
Social Studies Curriculum Leader for Hampton City
Schools, Ret., Hampton, VA
aha! Process Consultant

The Hurst-Bedford high schools are recognized, and in the state of Texas that's the second highest achievement [level]. We are recognized because of the work we do with data and our relationship piece with students.

HEB is a district of 25+ schools. Of those we have 19 elementaries, five junior highs, two high schools, and an alternative high school, and then we have an alternative elementary campus as well. We are a recognized district in Texas, and both our high schools are recognized, which is a phenomenal achieve-

ment in our area. And the only way we'd ever arrive with that is **by having a vertical, aligned process that works because I believe from pre-K we are preparing our children for college readiness or career readiness.** *And so it's an investment by everybody. Of our elementary campuses, we had 16 exemplary campuses out of the 19. The other two are recognized, and we had only one that was what we call acceptable, and that was by two students that we missed it. All our junior highs are exemplary, and we actually have two blue-ribbon schools now that are recognized, and they were honored in Washington, DC.*

—Karen Miller, Director of Continuous Improvement
and Professional Development
Hurst-Bedford Independent School District
Dallas/Ft. Worth, TX

Time, patience, **consistency with strategies,** *the structure of our school day, and our continuous working relationship with aha! Process have taken us to higher heights.*

—Lenisha Broadway
Principal, Ridgeroad Middle Charter School
North Little Rock, AR

One way that embedding Framework and School Improvement concepts changes a system is that it becomes proactive instead of reactive to a community, a setting, a problem. A second way we were able to impact the system is that we assisted people through the data. Facts drive actions, and so when you have data to drive your business, it makes you more credible. It also gives people a stronger sense of belonging, and it makes them feel the difference because they can see numbers change. Third, the School Improvement work builds intellectual capacity, not only in your students but in your staff. And when your staff and your students have intellectual capacity, your community has intellectual capacity.

Another place I saw a big change was in our exceptional student population with learning disabilities. When we instituted mental models into the teaching and learning, as well as their inclusion classes, we taught the students how to manipulate and use the mental models to their advantage in light of their learning styles. We taught the General Education teachers, along with the

Special Education teachers, how to facilitate the mental models. **At the end of the school year our General Education students at the secondary level made AYP—and 100% of our Exceptional Learner students made AYP.** *So the School Improvement process with mental models makes a difference—a huge difference.*

—Beverly Ray
aha! Process Consultant

Many of our teachers are first-generation college graduates, and so they were some of the first ones out of that poverty area and it really hit home to them (a) what they had accomplished and (b) **the power they had to help other children have that future story and to have those goals and dreams.** *So it was a very powerful day. It has already rippled through the district, and the best thing is that they want more information. It's not us forcing information onto them. They are clamoring for us to tell them more.*

—Linda Payne
Director of Professional Development in Testing for
Cabot Public Schools, Cabot, AR

From Understanding Poverty to Developing Human Capacity

Ruby Payne's Articles on Transforming Individuals, Families, Schools, Churches, and Communities

Ruby K. Payne, Ph.D.
   From Understanding Poverty to Developing Human Capacity: Ruby Payne's
   Articles on Transforming Individuals, Families, Schools, Churches, and
   Communities
   184 pp.

Copyright 2012 by aha! Process, Inc.
Published by aha! Process, Inc.

   For information, address
   aha! Process, Inc.
   P.O. Box 727
   Highlands, TX 77562-0727
   fax (281) 426-5600

   ISBN 13: 978-1-93458363-0
   ISBN 10: 1-934583-63-4

Copy editing by Dan Shenk
Book design by Paula Nicolella
Cover design by Dunn+Associates

Printed in the United States of America

From Understanding Poverty to Developing Human Capacity

Ruby Payne's Articles on Transforming Individuals, Families, Schools, Churches, and Communities

Ruby K. Payne, Ph.D.

Other Related Titles

School Improvement: 9 Systemic Processes
to Raise Achievement
(Payne & Magee)

Research-Based Strategies: Narrowing the Achievement
Gap for Under-Resourced Students
(Payne)

Removing the Mask: How to Identify and Develop
Giftedness in Students from Poverty
(Payne & Slocumb)

Under-Resourced Learners: 8 Strategies to
Boost Student Achievement
(Payne)

Bridges Out of Poverty: Strategies for Professionals
and Communities
(Payne, DeVol, & Dreussi-Smith)

Bridges to Sustainable Communities
(DeVol)

Getting Ahead in a Just-Gettin'-By World
(DeVol)

Investigations into Economic Class in America
(DeVol & Krodel)

Hidden Rules of Class at Work
(Payne & Krabill)

What Every Church Member Should Know About Poverty
(Payne & Ehlig)

Table of Contents

Nine Powerful Practices—Nine Strategies Help Raise the Achievement of Students Living in Poverty

First published in *Educational Leadership* 65(7), April 2008.

Sᴛᴜᴅᴇɴᴛs ꜰʀᴏᴍ ꜰᴀᴍɪʟɪᴇs ᴡɪᴛʜ ʟɪᴛᴛʟᴇ ꜰᴏʀᴍᴀʟ ᴇᴅᴜᴄᴀᴛɪᴏɴ often learn rules about how to speak, behave, and acquire knowledge that conflict with how learning happens in school. They also often come to school with less background knowledge and fewer family supports. Formal schooling, therefore, may present challenges to students living in poverty. Teachers need to recognize these challenges and help students overcome them. In my work consulting with schools that serve a large population of students living in poverty, I have found nine interventions particularly helpful in raising achievement for low-income students.

1. Build Relationships of Respect

Dr. James Comer (1995) puts it well: "No significant learning occurs without a significant relationship." Building a respectful relationship doesn't mean becoming the student's buddy. It means that teachers both insist on high-quality work and offer support. When my colleagues and I interviewed high school students in 1998 about what actions show that a teacher has respect for them, students identified the following:

- The teacher calls me by my name.
- The teacher answers my questions.

- The teacher talks to me respectfully.
- The teacher notices me and says "Hi."
- The teacher helps me when I need help.

The nonverbal signals a teacher sends are a key part of showing respect. I have found that when students feel they have been "dissed" by a teacher, they almost always point to nonverbals, rather than words, as the sign of disrespect. Nonverbal signals communicate judgment, and students can sense when a teacher's intent is to judge them rather than to offer support. Although it's hard to be conscious of nonverbal signals at times, one way to sense how you're coming across is to deeply question your intent. Your gestures and tone will likely reflect that intent.

2. Make Beginning Learning Relational

When an individual is learning something new, learning should happen in a supportive context. Teachers should help all students feel part of a collaborative culture. Intervene if you see an elementary student always playing alone at recess or a middle or high school student eating lunch alone. Assign any new student a buddy immediately and ensure that each student is involved with at least one extracurricular group at lunch or after school. Whenever possible, introduce new learning through paired assignments or cooperative groups.

3. Teach Students to Speak in Formal Register

Dutch linguist Martin Joos (1972) found that every language in the world includes five registers, or levels of formality: frozen, formal, consultative, casual, and intimate (see next page). Both school and work operate at the consultative level (which mixes formal and casual speech) and the formal level (which uses precise word choice and syntax). All people use the casual and intimate registers with friends, but students from families with little formal education may default to these registers. Researchers have found that the more generations a person lives in poverty, the less formal the register that person uses, with the exception of people from a strong religious background, who frequently encounter formal religious texts (Montana-Harmon, 1991). Hart and Risley's (1995) study of 42 families indicated that children living in families receiving welfare heard approximately 10 million words by age three, whereas children in families in which parents were classified as professional heard approximately 30 million words in the same period. Teachers conduct most tests through formal register, which puts poor students at a disadvantage. Teachers should address this issue openly and help students learn to communicate through consultative and formal registers. Some students may object that formal register is "white talk"; we tell them it's "money talk."

Figure 1. Levels of Formality of Language Level	Characteristics of Language
FROZEN	The words are always the same. Examples: The Lord's Prayer, The Pledge of Allegiance.
FORMAL	The word choice and sentence structure used by the business and education community. Uses a 1,200-word to 1,600-word spoken vocabulary. Example: "This assignment is not acceptable in its present format."
CONSULTATIVE	A mix of formal and casual register. Example: "I can't accept the assignment the way it is."
CASUAL	Language used between friends, which comes out of the oral tradition. Contains few abstract words and uses nonverbal assists. Example: "This work is a no-go. Can't take it."
INTIMATE	Private language shared between two individuals, such as lovers or twins.

Note. Dutch linguist Martin Joos (1972) identified these five levels of formality of language. Adapted from *A Framework for Understanding Poverty* (p. 27), by Ruby K. Payne, 1996, Highlands, TX: aha! Process. Copyright 1996 by aha! Process. Adapted with permission.

Have students practice translating phrases from casual into formal register. For example, a student I worked with was sent to the office because he had told his teacher that something "sucked." When I asked him to translate that phrase into formal register, he said, "There is no longer joy in this activity." Teachers should use consultative language (a mix of formal and casual) to build relationships and use formal register to teach content, providing additional explanation in consultative register.

4. Assess Each Student's Resources

One way to define poverty and wealth is in terms of the degree to which we have access to the following nine resources.

FINANCIAL
Having the money to purchase goods and services.

LANGUAGE
Being able to speak and use formal register in writing and in speech.

EMOTIONAL
Being able to choose and control emotional responses, particularly to negative situations, without engaging in self-destructive behavior. This is an internal resource and shows itself through stamina, perseverance, and choices.

MENTAL
Having the mental abilities and acquired skills (reading, writing, computing) to deal with daily life.

SPIRITUAL
Believing in divine purpose and guidance.

PHYSICAL
Having physical health and mobility.

SUPPORT SYSTEMS
Having friends, family, and backup resources available to access in times of need. These are external resources.

RELATIONSHIPS/ROLE MODELS
Having frequent access to adult(s) who are appropriate, who are **nurturing** to the child, and who do not engage in self-destructive behavior.

KNOWLEDGE OF HIDDEN RULES
Knowing the unspoken cues and habits of a group.

School success, as it's currently defined, requires a huge amount of resources that schools don't necessarily provide. Teachers need to be aware that many students identified as "at risk" lack these outside resources. Interventions that require students to draw on resources they do not possess will not work. For example, many students in households characterized by generational poverty have a very limited support system. If such a student isn't completing homework, telling that student's parent, who is working two jobs, to make sure the student does his or her homework isn't going to be effective. But if the school provides a time and place before school, after school, or during lunch for the student to complete homework, that intervention will be more successful.

5. Teach the Hidden Rules of School

People need to know different rules and behaviors to survive in different environments. The actions and attitudes that help a student learn and thrive in a low-income community often clash with those that help one get ahead in school. For example, when adult family members have little formal schooling, the student's environment may be unpredictable. Having reactive skills might be particularly important. These skills may be counterproductive in school, where a learner must plan ahead, rather than react, to succeed. If laughter is often used to lessen conflict in a student's community, that student may laugh when being disciplined. Such behavior is considered disrespectful in school and may anger teachers and administrators.

Educators often tell students that the rules they come to school with aren't valuable anywhere. That isn't true, and students know it. For example, to survive in many high-poverty neighborhoods, young people have to be able to fight physically if challenged—or have someone fight for them. But if you fight in school, you're usually told to leave.

The simple way to deal with this clash of norms is to teach students two sets of rules. I frequently say to students, You don't use the same set of rules in basketball that you use in football. It's the same with school and other parts of your life. The rules in school are different from the rules out of school. So let's make a list of the rules in school so we're sure we know them.

6. Monitor Progress and Plan Interventions

One teacher alone cannot address all students' achievement issues. Monitoring and intervening with at-risk kids must be a schoolwide process. Take the following steps:

- Chart student performance and disaggregate this data by subgroups and individuals.
- Keeping in mind your district's learning standards, determine which content you need to spend the most time on. Bloom (1976) found that the amount of time devoted to a content area makes a substantial difference in how well students learn that content. Set up a collaborative process for teachers to discuss learning standards and make these determinations.
- Plan to use the instructional strategies that have the highest payoff for the amount of time needed to do the activity. For example, teaching students to develop questions has a much higher payoff for achievement than completing worksheets.

- Use rubrics and benchmark tests to identify how well students are mastering standards; discuss the results.
- Identify learning gaps and choose appropriate interventions. Interventions can include scheduling extra instruction time, providing a supportive relationship, and helping students use mental models.
- Schedule these activities on the school calendar regularly.

7. Translate the Concrete into the Abstract

To succeed in school, students need to move easily from the concrete to the abstract. For example, a kindergarten teacher may hold up a real apple and tell students to find a drawing of an apple on a given page. Even though the two-dimensional apple on the page doesn't look like the real apple, students come to understand that the drawing represents the apple. In math, students need to understand that a numeral represents a specific number of items.

Teachers can help students become comfortable with the abstract representations characteristic of school by giving them mental models—stories, analogies, or visual representations. Mental models enable the student to make a connection between something concrete he or she understands and a representational idea. For example, in math, one can physically form a square with the number of items represented by any square number. We can teach students this concept quickly by drawing a box with nine X's in it. The student can visually see that 3 is the square root of 9, because no matter how the student looks at the model, there are 3 X's on each side.

Excellent teachers use mental models all the time, although they may not call them that. I have found that using mental models decreases the amount of time needed to teach and learn a concept.

8. Teach Students How to Ask Questions

When you have asked a student what part of a lesson he or she didn't understand, have you heard the reply, "All of it"? This response may indicate that the student has trouble formulating a specific question. Questions are a principal tool to gain access to information, and knowing how to ask questions yields a huge payoff in achievement (Marzano, 2007). In their research on reading, Palincsar and Brown (1984) found that students who couldn't ask good questions had many academic struggles.

To teach students how to ask questions, I assign pairs of students to read a text and compose multiple-choice questions about it. I give them sentence stems, such as "When _____ happened, why did _____ do _____?" Students develop questions using the stems, then come up with four answers to each question, only one of which they consider correct and one of which has to be funny.

9. Forge Relationships with Parents

Many low-income parents are so overwhelmed with surviving daily life that they can't devote time to their children's schooling. Even when time is available, the parent may not know how to support the child's learning.

It is essential to create a welcoming atmosphere at school for parents. Ask yourself these questions about the kind of experience parents have when they enter your building:

- How are parents usually greeted? With a smile, a command, a look, or the parent's name?
- What is the ratio of educators to parent in meetings? Six educators to one parent? Many parents experience such a situation as being "ganged up on." To avoid this perception, designate a person to greet the parent five minutes before the meeting starts and tell him or her who will be present and what is likely to happen. This is much better than having the parent walk into the room cold. When the meeting

is over, have all the educators leave the room (and don't have another obvious consultation in the parking lot). The person who met the parent ahead of time should walk the parent out of the building, ask how he or she is feeling, and find out whether the parent has more questions.

- Is the language used in parent meetings understandable, or is it "educationese"?
- Are parents often asked to make interventions they do not have the resources to make?
- Do parents realize that people at the school care about their children? Parents want to know first whether the school cares about and respects their child. Communicate this message early in the conference. It also helps to say, "We know that you care about your child, or you wouldn't be here."

I recommend doing home visits. Arrange to have a substitute for a particular day and send a letter home to a few parents saying that because teachers always ask parents to come to school, a pair of teachers would like to come by their house, say hello, and bring a gift. The gift should be something small, such as a magnet listing the school's name, phone number, and hours. If a parent wants to have an in-depth talk about the child, schedule a time that's good for both parties to talk further. Schools that have taken this approach, such as East Allen County Schools in Fort Wayne, Indiana, have strengthened the rapport between parents and teachers and lessened discipline referrals.

The Gift of Education

Educators can be a huge gift to students living in poverty. In many instances, education is the tool that gives a child life choices. A teacher or administrator who establishes mutual respect, cares enough to make sure a student knows how to survive school, and gives that student the necessary skills is providing a gift that will keep affecting lives from one generation to the next. Never has it been more important to give students living in poverty this gift.

References

Bloom, Benjamin. (1976). *Human characteristics and school learning.* New York, NY: McGraw-Hill Book Company.

Comer, James. (1995). Lecture given at Education Service Center, Region IV. Houston, TX.

Hart, Betty, & Risley, Todd R. (1995). *Meaningful differences in the everyday experience of young American children.* Baltimore, MD: Paul H. Brookes Publishing Co.

Joos, Martin. (1967). The styles of the five clocks. *Language and cultural diversity in American education.* (1972), Abrahams, R.D., & Troike, R.C. (Eds.). Englewood Cliffs, NJ: Prentice-Hall.

Marzano, Robert J. (2007). *The art and science of teaching: A comprehensive framework for effective instruction.* Alexandria, VA: Association for Supervision and Curriculum Development.

Palincsar, A. S., & Brown, A. L. (1984). The reciprocal teaching of comprehension-fostering and comprehension-monitoring activities. *Cognition and Instruction 1*(2), 117–175.

Payne, Ruby K. (1996, 2005). *A framework for understanding poverty* (5th ed.). Highlands, TX: aha! Process.

Payne, Ruby K. (2002). *Understanding learning* (2nd ed.). Highlands, TX: aha! Process.

Source: "Nine Powerful Practices," by Ruby Payne, 2008, *Educational Leadership 65*(7), pp. 48–52. © 2008 by ASCD. Reprinted with permission. Learn more about ASCD at www.ascd.org.

The Ten Dynamics of Poverty—By Understanding the Barriers Created by Poverty, Schools Can Help Overcome Them

First published in *Leadership Compass*, Summer 2009.
Reprinted with permission. Copyright 2009. National Association
of Elementary School Principals. All rights reserved.

MUCH DISCUSSION CENTERS AROUND THE BARRIERS that are created by poverty and those barriers' impact on school success. Arguments span the spectrum from "it is a system problem" to "it is a school problem" to "it is an individual problem." It would be myopic, in my view, to assign the blame solely to one cause. However, there are many things schools can do to make a difference in achievement. I would identify the following 10 dynamics:

1. RESOURCES OF THE HOUSEHOLD

Poor children are often defined almost exclusively by money. Actually, poverty is about access, or lack of access, to nine resources: financial, emotional, mental, spiritual, support systems, relationships/role models, knowledge of hidden rules, physical, and language. Resource analysis is important because it suggests where to make interventions, which work only if they're based on resources to which the student has access. For example, if the parent cannot read, there is no point in asking the parent to read to the child.

Schools can be much more successful if they know the resources of students, then base interventions on the available resources.

11

2. VOCABULARY/SECOND LANGUAGE LEARNERS

Hart and Risley (1995) found in their research that the average 4-year-old in a professional household has heard 45 million words while a 4-year-old in a welfare household has heard 13 million words. In fact, they found that a 3-year-old in a professional household has more vocabulary than an adult in a welfare household (Hart & Risley). Furthermore, Montano-Harmon (1991), a Latina linguist in California found that the issue for many bilingual children is that they know only casual register in both languages and do not know formal register (language of school and work) in either language.

Schools can be much more successful if they teach students to draw the meaning of vocabulary words and use discipline as an opportunity to teach formal register. (The student says something "sucks." The student needs to find two other ways to say sucks as a newscaster would say it—e.g., "There is no longer any joy in this activity.")

3. EXECUTIVE FUNCTION PROCESSING

In a study released in 2008 using EEG scans with poor and middle-class children, researchers found that the prefrontal cortex of the brain (executive function) in poor children was undeveloped and resembled the brains of adults who have had strokes (Kishiyama, Boyce, Jimenez, Perry, & Knight, in press). The executive function of the brain handles impulse control, planning, and working memory. The researchers went on to state that it is remediable, but there must be direct intervention.

Schools can direct teach planning and procedural steps and systematic processes (e.g., writing process, problem-solving process, etc.).

4. INTERGENERATIONAL TRANSFER OF KNOWLEDGE

Part of human capital is a knowledge base. Knowledge bases are a form of privilege, just as social access and money are. Such knowledge bases also can be passed on intergenerationally. In an Australian study that followed more than 8,500 children for 14 years, the researchers found they could predict with reasonable accuracy the verbal reasoning scores of 14-year-olds based on the maternal grandfather's occupation (Najman et al., 2004).

Schools can teach knowledge bases to students because knowledge is a form of power.

5. ABSTRACT REPRESENTATIONAL WORLD OF SCHOOL

Lave and Wenger (1991) indicate that beginning learning is about a situated environment that has people, relationships, context, tasks, and language. They add that when an individual makes the transition to formal schooling, learning becomes decontextualized. The context is taken away, relationships are seldom considered in the learning, and reasoning is not with stories but with laws and symbols (abstract representational systems). The research indicates that to make the transition between those two environments, one needs relationships and support systems.

Schools can use mental models (stories, analogies, drawings) to translate between the sensory world and the abstract representational world.

6. RELATIONSHIPS OF MUTUAL RESPECT

Because learning is always double-coded (Greenspan & Benderly, 1997)—both cognitively (based on the content) and emotionally (based on the relationship)—relationships enhance or detract from learning. Goleman (2006), in his book Social Intelligence, reports the findings of a study of 910 first-graders, all of whom had teachers with excellent pedagogy. However, if the at-risk students perceived the teacher as cold and controlling, the students essentially refused to learn from that teacher.

Schools can establish relationships of mutual respect with students and monitor for that through observation and student surveys. These are critical to learning.

7. DIFFERENCES BETWEEN SCHOOL RULES AND RULES OUTSIDE SCHOOL

Different environments require different responses. In the book A Framework for Understanding Poverty, these responses are referred to as "hidden rules." Because the worlds of work and school tend to use the same rules, if a student does not know the rules of school, then we teach those rules to that student. We use this analogy: Do you use the same rules in basketball that you do in football? The answer is no because you would lose. Different rules do not make one set better than another; they are just different. For example, if you are going to survive in a generational poverty neighborhood, you must know how to physically fight. But if you bring fighting into school, you are suspended or expelled.

Schools should teach the hidden rules of school to students so they also can negotiate the environments of school and work.

8. CHAOTIC, UNSAFE LEARNING ENVIRONMENT

Research on allostatic load indicates that the more chaotic (and dangerous) the environment, the less capable working memory is in the brain (McEwen, 2000). The more unstable the environment, the less learning occurs because time is given to surviving the current crisis, as opposed to devoting time to learning.

For brains to function well, schools must provide a strong classroom management approach, clear guidelines for behaviors, and a sense of safety, as well as teach two sets of rules and have relationships of mutual respect.

9. STAFF MOBILITY/STUDENT MOBILITY

High-poverty schools have high staff mobility and high student mobility. One of the characteristics of generational poverty is the amount of instability it brings to situations. In this case, the instability and insecurity occur both at home and at school. To combat high staff mobility, some school districts are offering a 5% additional pay differential to keep staff stable.

To combat high student mobility, it is imperative that schools use a formative assessment for students and immediately provide the interventions and safety nets for those students. See Payne (2008).

10. REALITIES OF GENERATIONAL POVERTY

There are many realities in generational poverty that impact children: gangs, violence, poor or no healthcare and dental care, substandard housing, greater environmental pollution, drugs, etc. While middle class may have some of these, generational poverty has a disproportionate amount—and at the same time there are fewer resources to address them.

Schools can provide access to community agencies that can also help students address these issues. See the book Collaboration For Kids (Conway, 2006), *which provides a process.*

Conclusion

While schools certainly cannot mitigate all the issues in poverty, schools *can* provide for many students from poverty the key tools to begin making the transition out of poverty, should those students wish to do so. Those tools include education, relationships with individuals different from oneself, and eventual employment. Such tools impact not just the generation being taught but the students' children and their grandchildren. Education is a gift for life.

References

Conway, H. W. (2006). *Collaboration for kids: Early-intervention tools for schools and communities.* Highlands, TX: aha! Process.

Goleman, D. (2006). *Social intelligence: The new science of human relationships.* New York, NY: Bantam.

Greenspan, S. I., & Benderly, B. L. (1997). *The growth of the mind and the endangered origins of intelligence.* Reading, MA: Addison-Wesley.

Hart, B., & Risley, T. R. (1995). *Meaningful differences in the everyday experience of young American children.* Baltimore, MD: P. H. Brookes.

Kishiyama, M. M., Boyce, W. T., Jimenez, A. M., Perry, L. M., & Knight, R. T. (in press). Socioeconomic disparities affect prefrontal function in children. Journal of Cognitive Neuroscience. Available from http://www.mitpressjournals.org/doi/abs/10.1162/jocn.2009.21101

Lave, J., & Wenger, E. (1991). *Situated learning: Legitimate peripheral participation.* New York, NY: Cambridge University Press.

McEwen, B. S. (2000). Allostasis and allostatic load: implications for neuropsychopharmacology. *Neuropsychopharmacology, 22*(2), 108–24.

Montano-Harmon, M. R. (1991). Discourse features of written Mexican Spanish: Current research in contrastive rhetoric and its implications. *Hispania, 74*(2), 417–425.

Najman, J. M., Aird, R., Bor, W., O'Callaghan, M., Williams, G. M., & Shuttlewood, G. J. (2004). The generational transmission of socioeconomic inequalities in child cognitive development and emotional health. *Social Science & Medicine, 58*(6), 1147–1158.

Payne, R. K. (2008). *Under-resourced learners: 8 strategies to boost student achievement.* Highlands, TX: aha! Process.

Advance: School Improvement—A Process to Use at the District/Campus Level

FOR ANY SCHOOL IMPROVEMENT PROCESS TO WORK in the complicated, crisis environment of the public school, it must have these characteristics:

1) Use a simpler process involving more people that takes less time.
2) Achieve critical mass of the staff in a short amount of time (so that everyone is moving in the same direction).
3) Have a method of monitoring each student for his/her learning progress.
4) Focus on calibrated student work* and the evaluation of that student work.

Many schools nowadays in the United States are making the following mistakes:

a) They are not tying all their accountability data to students but continue to focus on standards.

b) They are focusing huge amounts of time on teacher evaluation and lesson plans but not looking at calibrated student work/assignments. In other words, they are paying atten-

---

* Calibrated student work includes assignments and homework that is specifically leveled to a standard and level of evaluation.

tion to the teacher but not what the student is doing—primarily to test scores. It is analogous to evaluating a football coach by giving the players a paper/pencil test but never watching the players play a football game.

c) They have a grading/credit system separate from a state assessment system. Right now in most schools, grades are tied to assignments, weekly tests, and homework. Lesson plans are tied to standards and test scores. But they are not all tied together.

d) They are relying on programs rather than a process to track student learning

e) They are not tying student growth to the development of student expertise. (This is important in Texas because of the STAAR—State of Texas Academic Assessment Resource—assessment system now being implemented.)

f) Staff development is not tied to evaluating and calibrating student work against standards.

For example, to calibrate our high school work when I was a high school department chair in language arts, every English teacher took the SAT verbal test, and then we worked backwards by course by level to identify the work/assignments and evaluations that students would need to do in order to be ready for that test.

What follows is a process that can be used to get results. At aha! Process, we have used it in numerous schools to raise student achievement (and we continue to use it). Processes are much less expensive than programs and result in better achievement over time. Furthermore, processes become embedded into the daily life of the school rather than become additional tasks.

ADVANCE: SCHOOL IMPROVEMENT—the model we are currently using

	Process	Classroom Application
2 hours	Data analysis	Math—problem-solving model ELA (English/Language Arts)—nonfiction reading strategy and open-response strategy Share examples of walk-throughs
2 hours	Assigning time, aligning instruction *	Bellwork
2 hours	Assessment context, state assessment glossary, academic vocabulary, assessment blueprint	Word wall, vocabulary sketching (mental models) (Consultant needs time scheduled with principal to review assessment blueprint)
2 hours	Ten-question tests—first semester—by grading period: reading, writing, math (formative assessments)	Examples of mental models
2 hours	Interventions, data analysis, grade distribution, failure rate	Resource analysis and interventions
2 hours	Content comprehension—processes, step sheets, planning, RTI (response to intervention), specific mental models	Research-based strategies and targeted interventions using intervention form
2 hours	Ten-question tests—second semester—by grading period: reading, writing, math (formative assessments)	Question making
2 hours	Curriculum calibration, artifacts analysis, rubrics	Rubrics: ELA teachers teach writing rubric and open-response rubric to entire staff
2 hours	Voice, putting students in charge of their own learning, relational learning	Data conferencing with students Monitor for use of adult voice in classroom Monitor for examples of relational learning

* Needs to be done for each content area.

The left side of the grid is what needs to happen at the campus or secondary school department level. The right side of the grid is what needs to happen in the classroom. Each of the pieces of the process on the left-hand side of the grid constitutes two hours of staff development time, which is done with roving subs. If you have PLC (professional learning community) time, it can be used for this. For a detailed description, with administrator checklists included, see the book *School Improvement: 9 Systemic Processes to Raise Achievement* (www.ahaprocess.com).

THE 9 PROCESSES

If an instructional leader is going to get high student achievement, then he/she needs to know the following:

Step 1: Where are my students (by name) in relationship to our state accountability system? Many students count several times because they are in several categories. Accountability is a numbers and political game. It is about counting students in categories and determining ratios needed. (In our anecdotal data in many states across the USA, we find that you must have 80% of your students by subgroup in the top two categories of accountability rating in order to meet the state criteria for "meeting expectations" or "acceptable.")

Step 2: What are we teaching and how much time are we spending on that subject matter? Many instructional leaders can tell you about pedagogy but cannot tell you what the content is. Are the standards being taught?

Step 3: What specifically is the state testing? What is the vocabulary? What contexts will be used? For example, many secondary school language arts departments don't do any instruction in reading in tables, government documents, historical documents, technical writing, etc. Yet that context is on every state assessment.

Step 4: What is our own internal testing data telling us about student learning? What questions will we use each grading period to determine if we are making progress? Are these questions tied to the standards?

Step 5: Which students are not succeeding? What interventions do we need to try? What is the grade distribution? Too many failures? Grades too high? What are the resources that need to be augmented?

Step 6: How are we teaching the content so that it can be understood? All content, to be understood, requires a what (vocabulary), a why (purpose/application), and a how (processes). This is called content comprehension.

Step 7: What questions are we using for each grading period to monitor student progress against the standards?

Step 8: What are the assignments? Are the assignments calibrated to the standards?

Step 9: What are we doing to maintain relationships of mutual respect with students?

Steps 6 and 8 (content comprehension and calibration of student work) are critical and distinguishing steps of Advance and ones that many teachers may find challenging.

WHAT IS CONTENT COMPREHENSION?

Just as reading comprehension means you understand the reading passage, so content comprehension means you understand the content at a level where you can manipulate it and use it.

To use and manipulate content, in addition to knowing the meaning of vocabulary, you also must know the purpose, structures, patterns, and processes used in that particular discipline or content. These four factors tell you what is more important and less important as you sort information in order to use it.

For example, the purpose of language arts is to study how structure and language are used to influence a reader. It is basically about writers and readers. The structures are the genres (short story, drama, poetry, biography, novels, etc.), grammar, organizational patterns of text, syllables, phonics, etc. The patterns then become units of study. The processes can include reading, writing, speaking, filmmaking, and listening. So an expert teacher in language arts is going to help his/her students understand that language arts is always about the relationship between reader and writer—the manipulations of structure, word choice, organization, etc.—in that process.

Another example: Math is about assigning order and value to the universe. We use numbers, space, and time as primary structures to do that. Patterns that are taught include fractions (part to whole of space), decimals (part to whole of numbers), and measurement (assigning the value of space and time). Processes are addition, subtraction, multiplication, and division. So an elementary school teacher would facilitate a discussion with students about how to know how much space is theirs in a classroom before introducing fractions. The class would measure the room, divide it with masking tape, and calculate space using fractions. The teacher could do the same thing by dividing pizza. The students would then understand what each student needs to know about measurement and fractions.

For example, the purpose of chemistry is to understand chemical bonding. The periodic table provides the rules or patterns for bonding. The process used to figure out the bonding is equations. The structure theory has varied from shell theory to vapor cloud theory to string theory.

When students have content comprehension, teachers can spend the majority of their time teaching the use and manipulation of the content. For example, in language arts in high school, the teacher does not test by asking what color the girl's dress was in the story, but rather "What specific techniques did the writer use to make the reader feel empathetic toward the girl?" Or: "How would the reader have felt different if this short story had been told in a poem?"

Lee Shulman found that this was a critical issue in excellent teaching. Furthermore, he indicated that graphic visual representations (mental models) used by the teacher came out of this understanding—and that teachers then knew when a student had a slight misunderstanding versus no understanding at all.

And it also can be stated that if teachers don't understand their content against these four criteria—purpose, structures, patterns, and processes—they can't facilitate or develop high achievement. It isn't possible to teach what you don't know.

CALIBRATION OF STUDENT WORK

Current practice is to look primarily at teacher lesson plans. All teacher lesson plans tell you is what the teacher intended to teach. They don't tell you what the student learned.

TEACHER LESSON PLAN

OBJECTIVE: Students will understand the events preceding the U.S. Civil War.

TEXT: Chapter 16 in the textbook.

OPENING ACTIVITY: Break students into pairs. Have them read Chapter 16 and take notes.

ASSIGNMENT: Students will answer the questions at the end of the chapter.

STUDENT ASSESSMENT: Students did the assignment and answered the questions correctly at least 80% of the time.

A first step in understanding what the student learned is to focus on student assignments, how those assignments are calibrated to the standards. This process of focusing on student work can be taught to every teacher.

WHAT MIGHT A CALIBRATED ASSIGNMENT BE IN 11TH-GRADE SOCIAL STUDIES?

ASSIGNMENT

Given that personalities and timing always play a key role in history, discuss the personalities of Robert E. Lee, his second in command, and Jeb Stuart. All were preoccupied with personal issues. For each personality, identify the preoccupation. Discuss how these preoccupations, in conjunction with the timing of the war, contributed to the outcome of the Civil War.

Compare these factors to a current situation in politics in the United States. How do preoccupations of personal issues and timing contribute to historical outcomes?

EVALUATION OF ABOVE ASSIGNMENT

This response has four parts:

1. Analysis of the personalities and their preoccupations (30% of grade)
2. Contribution of their personalities and timing to the outcome of the war (30% of grade)
3. Comparison to a current situation in the United States (20% of grade)
4. Comments on how personal issues and timing contribute to outcomes (20% of grade)

Contrast this assignment to the commonly used practice of having students answer the questions at the end of the chapter or using paper/pencil tests as the primary means of assessment. This process is one that will make a significant difference in student learning.

CONCLUSION

If a campus or department systemically follows this process, it will have addressed issues necessary for high student performance. It will have:

1) Used a simpler process that involves more people that takes less time.
2) Achieved critical mass of the staff in a short amount of time (so that everyone is moving in the same direction).
3) Monitored each student for his/her learning progress.
4) Focused on calibrated student work* and the evaluation of that student work.

These factors make a significant difference for teachers and students.

RESULTS

Please see the Appendix for more detail about two schools districts that have successfully used the aha! Process School Improvement Process to raise the achievement of their students. The first is Lowndes County Schools in Mississippi, and the second is Ridge Road Middle Charter School in North Little Rock, Arkansas.

Using the aha! Process School Improvement Model beginning in 2009, West Lowndes Elementary has increased achievement over time and is outperforming a control group in literacy and math.

West Lowndes Elementary (WLE) students have demonstrated language arts and mathematics gains over time. Data in this report find that third-grade students realized gains of 26.1% in language arts and 31.5% in math from 2008 to 2011. WLE fourth-grade students realized gains of 35.7% and 40.7%, respectively, in language arts and math, while fifth-grade students realized gains of 3.6% in language arts and 16.6% in math during the 2008–11 time span.

Furthermore, these students outperformed control-group students at a school with similar demographics. The third-graders outperformed their control-group counterparts by 36.4% and 25.7%, respectively, in language arts and math, while fourth-graders outperformed the control group by 32.6% in language arts and 36% in math, and fifth-graders outperformed the control group by 18.6% in language arts and 30.7% in math, according to the 2011 test scores reported for the Mississippi Curriculum Tests, 2nd Edition. For more detail and findings for West Lowndes Middle School, see the full report in the Appendix.

At Ridgeroad Middle Charter School (RRMCS), aha! Process began its work in 2003–04 after the school became a conversion charter school. In addition to the following results, notable gains (as shared by the principal at the time, Lenisha Broadway) showed an increase of students scoring proficient in Algebra I from 78% in 2007 to 97% in 2010 and 84% in geometry in 2007 to 100% in proficient in 2010. Other findings from the data:

- Seventh- and eighth-grade students at RRMCS have demonstrated literacy and mathematics gains over time. Data in this report find that seventh-grade students realized gains of 8% in literacy and 14% in math between 2005–06 and 2008–09. RRMCS eighth-graders realized gains of 5% and 13%, respectively, in literacy and math during the same time span.

- Furthermore, these students outperformed control-group students at a school with similar demographics. Seventh-graders outperformed their control-group counterparts by 7% and 14%, respectively, in literacy and math, while eighth-graders outperformed the control group by 17% in literacy and 9% in math, according to the 2008–09 test scores reported for the ABE (Augmented Benchmark Exam).

- When looking collectively at the seventh- and eighth-grade students eligible for free/reduced lunch, these students show consistent gains over time, increasing achievement in literacy by 15.5% and in mathematics by 28.5%, according to a comparison of 2005–06 test results with those reported in 2008–09.

- Finally, an impact on overall school climate can be seen in the reduction of teacher turnover from 40% in 2003–04 to 10% in 2007–08. Teacher mobility was cited by RRMCS as a barrier to student success. As a result of the partnership between RRMCS and aha! Process, this barrier has been dramatically lowered.

For even more information on results of the aha! Process school improvement work, see the full report in the Appendix and/or visit our website at http://www.ahaprocess.com/School_Programs/ ResearchResults/.

Effectively Communicating Standards to Parents—Standards Must Be in Lay Terms and Demonstrated to Parents in Order for Them to Understand How Their Children Are Doing

First published (excerpt) in *Leadership Compass,* Winter 2006. Reprinted with permission. Copyright 2006. National Association of Elementary School Principals. All rights reserved.

A S U.S. EDUCATION INCREASINGLY MOVES toward standards-based reporting, teaching and learning become much more diagnostic. This is a major paradigm shift for schools because we have always been so programmatic in orientation. We talk about how children are doing in relationship to a program but not how they're doing in relationship to themselves or against a set of criteria, e.g., in such-and-such a chapter in math, division, she had 75 out of 100 problems correct. Standards-based reporting requires a *diagnostic approach* that looks at how students are l*earning in relationship to a set of criteria* and *not a program,* e.g., what part of division does he understand and not understand?

Therefore, many districts and principals are struggling with communicating student progress to parents against standards. When the standards are given to parents, many times the standards are not understood because they are in "educationese." So parents are baffled, and teachers are overwhelmed.

This article will give some specific guidelines to consider and some specific examples of how to communicate with parents.

There are three issues: (1) how to communicate the standards in lay terms, (2) what parents need to know versus what they want to know, and (3) how to show parents the relationship between standards and student progress/success.

PERSONALIZING STANDARDS

The simplest way to address all three is to use the child as the focus and embed the standards underneath that development. In other words, what behaviors will children exhibit when they have mastered the standards—and how do you know where they are in the mastery. All most parents really want to know is this: *Tell me about my child and his/her relationship to growth and the continuum of development.*

The guidelines then for communicating standards consist of the following:

1) Keep it simple (front and back of one page for reading—and same for math).
2) Translate the information directly to what the child will do. In other words, rather than state the standard, you state the standard as a behavior or attribute of the child, e.g., "He can tell a story from pictures."
3) Make available the list of standards keyed to what the student can do for the benefit of those parents who request that, as well as for teacher reference.
4) Show the progression and development of the acquisition of the standard in relationship to what the child will do. It gives parents a sense of how to help their child if they so desire.
5) Include student work and examples so parents can make their own determinations as well (see following example about kindergarten writing).

WHAT DOES IT LOOK LIKE?

For example: reading. Every state has a standard that students will be able to read and comprehend. What does that mean to parents? How do they know where their child is on the continuum? Many districts have a check-off list with "[name] is below expectations, meets expectations, is above expectations." But what does that mean? And where does a parent go with that information? A numerical grade may be even less helpful.

To communicate to parents, I wrote this basic rubric that was then refined by a group of teachers to the current example. The research on skilled readers (*Becoming a Nation of Readers*) is that they have five characteristics. They:

1) Are fluent (i.e., they can decode)
2) Are motivated (they actually do read)
3) Are constructive (they comprehend and make meaning)
4) Use a process (they predict, sort, summarize, conclude)
5) Are strategic (they can fix their understandings and misunderstandings)

We used these rubrics for parent/teacher conferences in October, then again at the end of the school year. The teacher used one color highlighter to indicate where the student was performing in October and a different color in May. This also allowed the parent to see the growth. We put it on the front and back of cardstock so it was only one sheet. Then it became part of the permanent record.

How does this rubric convey standards? It is in lay language. It gives the parent an understanding of where the child is, what the child needs to do to progress, and what the expectations are. A teacher can say, "It is our expectation that every student be at the *capable* level and our goal is to have everyone at the *expert* level for his/her grade level."

And it's in simple language, translated directly to the child. The standards are embedded into the complete rubric without taking away the focus from the child. The teacher can then show the parent an example of a story that the students are expected to be able to read. Depending on the educational level of the parent, the language of this rubric can be simplified more. (You have my permission to adapt, copy, use, and change these rubrics.)

Reading Rubric: Grade 1

Student name:_____ School year:_____

Campus:_____ Grade:_____

	Beginning	Developing	Capable	Expert
Fluent	Decodes words haltingly	Decodes sentences haltingly	Knows vowel teams (*ea, ee, oa,* etc.)	Decodes polysyllabic words
	Misses key sounds	Knows conditions for long vowels (vowel at end of syllable, e.g., *me, he*)	Identifies common spelling patterns	Decodes words in context of paragraph
	Identifies most letter sounds	Identifies blends and consonants	Uses word-attack skills to identify new words	Decodes words accurately and automatically
	Identifies short vowels	Decodes digraphs and *r*-control vowels (*or, ar, er,* etc.)	Reads sentences in meaningful sequence	Reads paragraphs in meaningful sequence
	Says/ recognizes individual words	Reads at rate that does not interfere with meaning	Reads with expression	Reads with expression, fluency, appropriate tone, and pronunciation
Construc-tive	Predictions are incomplete, partial, and unrelated	Predicts what might happen next	Predicts story based on pictures and other clues	Can predict possible endings to story with some accuracy
	Predictions indicate no or inappropriate prior knowledge	Makes minimal links to personal experience/prior knowledge	Relates story to personal experience/prior knowledge	Can compare/ contrast story with personal experience

continued on next page

continued from previous page

	Beginning	Developing	Capable	Expert
Motivated	Does not read independently	Reads when teacher or parent requests	Will read for specific purpose	Self-initiates reading
	Concentrates on decoding	Eager to utilize acquired skills (words and phrases)	Uses new skills frequently in self-selected reading	Reads for pleasure
Strategic	Does not self-correct	Recognizes mistakes but has difficulty in self-correcting	Has strategies for self-correction (reread, read ahead, ask questions, etc.)	Analyzes self-correction strategies as to best strategy
	Uncertain as to how parts of story fit together	Can identify characters and setting in story	Can identify characters, settings, and events of story	Can talk about story in terms of problem and/or goal
Process	Cannot tell what has been read	Does not sort important from unimportant	Can determine with assistance what is important and unimportant	Organizes reading by sorting important from unimportant

Reading Rubric: Grade 2

Student name:_____   School year:_____

Campus:_____ Grade:_____

	Beginning	Developing	Capable	Expert
Fluent	Misses key phonemic elements	Knows basic phonetic structure of vowels: short, long, r-control, vowel teams	Uses word-attack skills to identify new words in section	Decoding not an issue; it is taken for granted
	Rate of reading interferes with meaning	Occasionally rate of reading interferes with meaning	Says sentences in meaningful sequence	Analyzes selection and uses most effective reading rate
	New vocabulary impairs understanding	Mispronounces unfamiliar words	Uses contextual clues to determine pronunciation of new words	Enjoys new words and practices using them in his/her vocabulary
Construc-tive	Makes some use of clues to determine what text will be about	Can predict what character might do next	Can predict possible outcomes from selection	Connects personal experience to predict outcomes
	May mention character he/she read about previously	Remembers general characters but not detail	Can identify main character	Can give detailed accounting of character and motive
	Skips over new words	New vocabulary impairs understanding	For new word, can give example but not definition	Can generate definition or synonym for new word

continued on next page

continued from previous page

	Beginning	Developing	Capable	Expert
Motivated	Has limited interaction with or response to reading	May be involved in or identify with portion of story	Responds on personal basis to selection	Tells others about what he/she has read
	Reads only when asked	Self-initiates reading	Has criteria for selecting reading materials	Analyzes personal choices and determines new selections to explore
Strategic	Is uncertain as to how all parts fit together but can identify parts of selections	Has structure for story reading	Understands criteria of expository piece	Differentiates fiction from non-fiction by structure of piece
Process				
Before	Simply begins reading; does not know purpose	Has purpose for reading but relies heavily on pictures	Demonstrates some knowledge of clues to use before reading (looks at graphics, predicts, asks questions)	Applies strategies before reading that help better understand what text will be about
During	Keeps reading if he/she does not understand	Has only external strategies (will ask for help)	Uses some strategies during reading *	Applies appropriate strategies while reading; can self-correct **
After	Cannot verbalize what he/she read	Can identify which part he/she liked best	Can summarize with assistance/direction	Summarizes accurately

* Reading strategies: Summarizes, retells events; makes mental picture of what author says; predicts next event; alters predictions based on new information.

** Self-correction or "fix-up" strategies: Looks back, looks ahead, rereads, slows down, asks for help.

Reading Rubric: Grade 3

Student name:_____   School year:_____

Campus:_____   Grade:_____

	Beginning	Developing	Capable	Expert
Fluent	Mispronounces common words	Sees word root and endings separately	Understands that prefixes, roots, and suffixes are "changeable parts"	Analyzes pronunciation using analogy to known words and word parts
	Decodes sentences haltingly	Decodes words accurately and automatically	Decodes words in context of paragraph	Reads with expression, fluency, and appropriate tone and pronunciation
Constructive	New vocabulary impairs understanding	Can generate an example or synonym for new word	Can generate synonyms, definition, or antonym for new word	Uses new and unusual words in writing or speaking
	Predicts story based on pictures and other clues	Identifies parts of story in relation to his/her own experience	Connects personal experience to clues and text	Can compare and contrast previous personal experience to parts of story
Motivated	Reading is initiated by teacher	Reading is initiated by student	Reads for pleasure	Reads for pleasure and information as needed
	Holds as much beginning information as possible and forgets rest	May describe what selection is about and provide some detail	Identifies main idea	Identifies main idea and supporting information
	Does not read for information	Reads for information if teacher-initiated	Uses appropriate text for needed information	Compares/ contrasts one piece of reading with/to another

continued on next page

continued from previous page

	Beginning	Developing	Capable	Expert
Strategic	Has difficulty differentiating important from unimportant	Knows important parts exist but cannot always identify	Can identify important information	Can identify and store important information and discard unimportant
	Does not self-correct	Recognizes mistakes but has difficulty in self-correcting	Has strategies for self-correction **	Analyzes self-correction strategies as to best strategy
Process				
Before	Prereading strategies involve number of pages and size of print	Identifies purpose for reading	Identifies purpose and applies strategies before reading that help better understand what text will be about	Determines strategies needed to understand selection
During	Calls words and skips words if they cannot be understood or pronounced	Some aspects of text are connected to prior knowledge/ experience	Uses some strategies during reading *	Applies appropriate strategies while reading; can self-correct **
After	Summaries are retelling of as much as is remembered	Needs help with summary; can identify which part he/she liked best	Has strategy for categorizing and summarizing information	Organizes reading by sorting important from unimportant and relating it to purpose and structure

* Reading strategies: Summarizes, retells events, makes mental picture of what author says; predicts next event, alters predictions based on new information.
** Self-correction or "fix-up" strategies: Looks back, looks ahead, rereads, slows down, asks for help.

Reading Rubric: Grade 4

Student name:_____ School year:_____

Campus:_____ Grade:_____

	Beginning	Developing	Capable	Expert
Fluent	Mispronounces common words	Sees word root and ending separately	Understands that prefixes, roots, and suffixes are "changeable parts"	Analyzes pronunciation using analogies to known words and word parts
	Decodes words haltingly	Decodes words in context of paragraph	Decoding is non-issue	Reads with expression, fluency, and appropriate tone and pronunciation
Construc-tive	Can predict what character might do next	Can predict possible endings to story	Can predict more than one ending/solution	Can predict endings to story and explain advantages and disadvantages for author in using various endings
	New vocabulary impairs understanding	Can generate example or synonym for new word	Can generate synonyms, definition, or antonyms for new word	Uses new vocabulary in writing or speaking
Motivated	Little understanding of reason for reading	Reads text because teacher said to	Establishes clear purpose for reading	Evaluates purpose for reading
	Limited interaction with or response to reading	May mention character he/she has read about previously	Compares/contrasts one piece of reading with/to another	Analyzes personal choices and determines new selections to explore

continued on next page

continued from previous page

	Beginning	**Developing**	**Capable**	**Expert**
Strategic	Does not have enough information to ask questions	Has difficulty asking questions	Can ask questions about what was read	Asks questions that tie this text and other reading together
	Has difficulty differentiating important from unimportant	Can use structures to identify important information	Uses structures to assign order, remember characters, and identify problem/goal	Uses structure to determine most important aspects of text to remember
	Has some difficulty differentiating structure of fiction from non-fiction	Differentiates fiction from non-fiction by structure of piece	Can differentiate among structures used in fiction ***	Can differentiate among non-fiction structures ****
Process				
Before	Prereading strategies involve number of pages and size of print	Identifies purpose for reading	Applies strategies before reading that help him/her better understand what text will be about	Determines strategies needed to better understand selection
During	Calls words and skips words if not understood	Some aspects of text are connected to prior knowledge/experience	Uses some strategies during reading *	Applies appropriate strategies while reading; can self-correct **
After	Summaries are retelling of as much as is remembered	Can identify part he/she likes best but needs help with summary	Has strategy for categorizing information	Organizes reading by sorting important from unimportant and relating it to purpose and structure

* Reading strategies: Summarizes, retells events, makes mental picture of what author says, predicts next event, alters predictions based on new information.
** Self-correction or "fix-up" strategies: Looks back, looks ahead, rereads, slows down, asks for help.
*** Fiction structure (examples): Flashbacks, chronological, episodic, story within story.
**** Non-fiction structure (examples): Topical, cause and effect, sequential, comparison/contrast, persuasive.

Reading Rubric: Grade 5

Student name:_____ School year:_____

Campus:_____ Grade:_____

	Beginning	Developing	Capable	Expert
Fluent	Rate of reading interferes with meaning	Occasionally rate of reading interferes with meaning	Analyzes selection and uses most effective reading rate	Can articulate the demands of the reading task
Construc-tive	Has trouble understanding meaning of text	Can understand text but has difficulty formulating questions	Can explain why text is important and can summarize main points	Assigns meaning and relates information in a larger context of knowledge
	Vocabulary slows reader	Can use text to make meaning of new vocabulary	Can ask questions over text	Vocabulary applied outside of text and used to refine understanding
Motivated	Does not read for information; concentrates on decoding	Holds as much beginning information as possible and forgets rest	Identifies main idea; determines fact from non-fact	Identifies main idea; determines fact from non-fact
	Can provide some details about selection	May describe what selection is about and provide some detail	Compares and contrasts information to other events or experiences	Compares and contrasts information to other events or experiences
	Reading is initiated by teacher	Reading is initiated by student	Shares reading with others	Shares reading with others

continued on next page

continued from previous page

	Beginning	Developing	Capable	Expert
Strategic	Differentiates fiction from non-fiction by structure of piece	Can differentiate among structures used in fiction ***	Can differentiate among non-fiction structures ****	Can articulate and analyze author's use of structure
Sorting	Can remember some of important pieces	Uses structures to assign order, remember characters, and identify problem/goal	Uses structures to determine most important aspects of text to remember	Discusses how structures assist reader in sorting important from unimportant
Asks questions	Does not have enough information to ask questions	Has difficulty asking questions	Can ask questions about what was read	Asks questions that tie this text to others
Self-correction strategies	Does not self-correct	Recognizes mistakes but has difficulty self-correcting	Has strategies for self-correction **	Analyzes self-correction strategies as to best strategy **
Identifies purpose	Little understanding of reason for reading	Reads text because teacher said to	Establishes clear purpose for reading	Evaluates purpose for reading

continued on next page

continued from previous page

	Beginning	Developing	Capable	Expert
Process				
Before	Does not predict	Has some difficulty making predictions	Applies strategies before reading that help better understand what text will be about	Predicts and identifies how author or genre tends to end selections
During	Keeps reading if he/she does not understand	Uses some strategies during reading *	Applies appropriate strategies while reading; can self-correct **	Analyzes own reading and thinking while reading
After	Summaries are retelling of as much as is remembered	Has strategy for categorizing information	After reading, revises schema/ conceptual organization	Develops more clarity in thinking as result of reading

* Reading strategies: Summarizes, retells events, makes mental picture of what author says, predicts next event, alters predictions based on new information.
** Self-correction or "fix-up" Strategies: Looks back, looks ahead, rereads, slows down, asks for help.
*** Fiction structures (examples): Flashbacks, chronological, episodic, story within story.
**** Non-fiction structures (examples): Topical, cause and effect, sequential, comparison/ contrast, persuasive.

AN ADDITIONAL TOOL

An additional tool that we used to convey this information to parents was in writing for kindergarten. We explained that oral language preceded written language—and provided the rubric below. In addition, we provided samples of what that actually looked like for kindergartners. Parents can then be given a sample of their own child's work and determine where the child is developmentally.

	Scribble/ Drawing Prephonemic	Early Prephonemic	Phonemic	Standard
Oral Fluency	Talks about characters Response may ramble May tell a part of story Includes irrelevant information	Can tell a story witha beginning, middle, and end	Gives details about the characters and has a meaningful story	Has a richly developed story with detailed characters and unusual word choice
Written Fluency	Use drawings and scribbles to resemble written form Left to right progression not evident	Draws pictures and writes a series of letters that resemble a sentence or compelte thought	Writing resembles specific words Uses invented spellings The story can be ascertained	The story has several sentences with more stand spellings and makes sense
Elaboration	Detail in pictures Details may be confused	Detail in oral language	Used pictures and language for details in writing	Uses language for details in writing

Developmental Stages in Writing/Spelling

I.   Scribble, Drawing, and Prephonemic

   ■ represents words, sentences or stories

(That's Daddy)

   ■ string of letters to represent sounds (words or sentences)

M E s

tomato

II.   Early Phonemic

   ■ representation of sentences with one or two letters

t b V

(It is his birthday)

   ■ representation of words initial consonants

G

(Grass)

(are)

Developmental Stages in Writing/Spelling

■ representation of words with initial final consonants

PNM_T = punishment
SM_T = cement
$V\c{V}$ = vacation
$M\l N$ = motion
OS_N = ocean

III.   Phonemic

■ representation of words with initial, final and interior vowel

G S

(Grass)

■ representation of words with initial, final and interior consonants, and vowel place holder. Vowel may be incorrect but in correct position

Gres

(Grass)

IV.   Standard or Conventional Spelling

■ representation of word with final components of visual memory systems and vowel discrimination

Grass

(Grass)

Conclusion:

If children at the different stages of writing are forced to perform in a conventional way, they often become confused and are prevented from developing naturally to a higher level. As a teacher, accept young children's early writing with the understanding that they will develop to higher levels as they experience authentic written language in a community of readers and writers.

February 19, 1993
cwo

Scribble/Drawing Prephonemic Stage

This is a good representation of a child's attempt to scribble/write and orally describe his thoughts. The word cat was copied from the board, further illustrating his correction of letters and to words and writing.

Scribble/Drawing Stage

This child is in the scribble/drawing stage of development. His description of the picture represents his first attempt to connect symbols with words. He conveys his ideas through oral compositon and drawing.

Early Phonemic

The student has the concept of a sentence but not necessarly the concept of a story. The pictures help explain the facts. The notion of sequence is absent.

Phonemic

The student is able to order sentences in a sequence that has meaning. Emergent writers often use repetitive patterns. Writing is based on creative meaning.

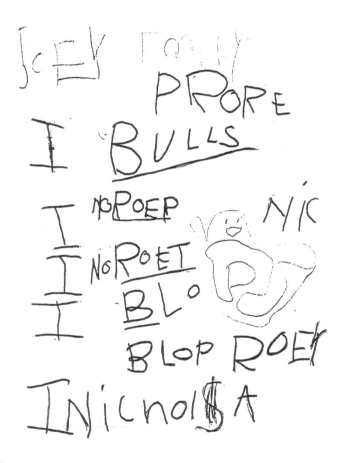

Phonemic

This piece has format and structure. The student understands that words go in an order in sequence and that they often go around a picture.

WHAT DO YOU DO FOR PARENTS WHO DON'T SPEAK ENGLISH? HOW DO YOU CONVEY STANDARDS TO ALL PARENTS?

The same rubrics are used. Either the child or a translator shows the parent what the child can do and what the expectations are. Another mechanism is to explain it and have it translated in the language the parents speak. You can then have it downloadable for iPods or press it to a CD or DVD. (If you go to Apple's *iTunes University,* you can list free downloadable files.) Virtually every home in poverty has a CD player or DVD player. So you can video it. It's highly beneficial if you video the child and record at school on the school computers, save it to DVD or CD, and have the child take it home and the parents view it.

SHOULD YOU INVOLVE STUDENTS IN THE DISCUSSION WITH PARENTS?

Beginning in third grade, it's a good idea for students to be involved and be able to explain to their parents where they are on the continuum of standards acquisition. After all, it is the students' learning—and if students aren't cognizant where they are in the learning, then they don't know what the expectations are either.

IN CONCLUSION

All most parents ever really want to know is *how my child is doing overall, and how he/she is doing in relationship to other children and the expectations.* When you provide the tools for parents to know the continuum and the expectations, they also can place their child on the continuum of development. When it's given in language the parents can understand and the focus is on the child, then the standards can easily be understood.

Bibliography

Bloom, Benjamin. (1976). *Human characteristics and school learning.* New York, NY: McGraw-Hill Book Company.

Caine, Renate Nummela, & Caine, Geoffrey. (1991). *Making connections: Teaching and the human brain.* Alexandria, VA: Association of Supervision and Curriculum Development.

Calallen Middle School. Calallen Independent School District. (1998). Corpus Christi, TX.

Eisner, Elliott, & Vallance, Elizabeth. (1974). *Conflicting conceptions of curriculum.* Berkeley, CA: McCutchan Publishing.

Feuerstein, Reuven, et al. (1980). *Instrumental enrichment: An intervention program for cognitive modifiability.* Glenview, IL: Scott, Foresman & Company.

Gerzon, Mark. (1996). *A house divided.* New York, NY: Putnam Publishing Company.

Glickman, Carl, Jordan, Stephan P., & Ross-Gordon, Jovita M. (1997). *Supervision of instruction: A developmental approach* (4th ed.). New York, NY: Allyn & Bacon.

Goose Creek Consolidated Independent School District. (1990). Baytown, TX (work shared by district math team).

Goose Creek Consolidated Independent School District. (1994). Baytown, TX (work done in collaboration with Ruby K. Payne).

http://intranet.cps.k12.il.us/Assessments/Ideas_and_Rubrics/Rubric_Bank/MathRubrics.pdf

Idol, Lorna, & Jones, B. F. (Eds.). (1991). *Educational values and cognitive instruction: Implications for reform.* Hillsdale, NJ: Lawrence Erlbaum Associates.

Joyce, Bruce, & Showers, Beverly, & Rolheiser-Bennett, Carol. (1987, October). Staff development and student learning: a synthesis of research on models of teaching. *Educational Leadership.*

Lezotte, Lawrence W. (1992). *Creating the total quality effective school.* Okemos, MI: Effective Schools Products.

Runyan Elementary School. Conroe Independent School District. (1996). Conroe, TX (work done in collaboration with Ruby K. Payne).

www.indep.k12.mo.us/pdc/MAPS/Math8/math_rubric.htm%2copy

www.laramie1.k12.wy.us/instruction

www.laramie1.k12.wy.us/instruction/math/benchmarkmath.htm

Six Basic Components of Classroom Discipline and Management

First published in *Instructional Leader,* January 2007.
Reprinted with permission. *Instructional Leader* is produced by the
Texas Elementary Principals and Supervisors Association. © 2012.

ARE YOU HAVING DIFFICULTY KEEPING your beginning teachers? Are your veteran teachers having difficulty with today's students? Are your beginning teachers struggling with discipline? Do you have days when the discipline issues are overwhelming?

Today's classroom and campus require a systemic approach. It is no longer enough to think about them as isolated places. The classroom is a manifestation of the larger societal issues and must be addressed differently.

A principal can insist that six basic components of that system are in place. The basic components are examined below.

1 CLASSROOMS AND CAMPUSES ARE SYSTEMS

Classrooms and campuses are systems. If you want to have good discipline, then think of your campus and classrooms as a system— and manage it as a system.

Think of it as a highway system with stoplights, intersecting roads, rules about turning, staying in the proper lane, etc. If we didn't have a system for highways and roads, driving would be impossible—or at least impossibly dangerous. Even when you know the system for driving and highways, you still have to watch each driver. But without a system, it would be total chaos. Likewise, campuses and classrooms must have a system.

Therefore, *within your classroom,* your system would do well to include the following:

	ON THE HIGHWAY	IN YOUR CLASSROOM
PROCEDURES	Which lane you are in, who goes first at a stop sign, etc.	How do students pass out papers? How do students put materials away?
RULES	When you stop and go, who has the right of way, etc.	What happens if a student cheats? If a cell phone rings during class? If a student curses? Etc.
MOTIVATION (consequences and rewards)	What motivates me to drive well? Example: tickets, lower insurance rates for good driving, jail, etc.	What would motivate students to learn and behave?
ORGANIZATION AND PLANNING	Which is the best route to use? What do I need to take?	When are assignments due? How do students control impulsivity?
SCHEDULES	When do I need to leave to get there on time? Where do I need to go today?	What time does this subject or class start? What will happen next? When do students go to the next center or class?
PARTICIPANTS	Other drivers: How do all the drivers travel safely in the same space?	Students: How does a group of students work together safely and productively?
PERSON IN CHARGE	My driving: Am I aggressive, engaged in road rage, distracted by my cell phone?	Teacher: What is my approach to students when I discipline them?

Not using a systemic approach is like driving without knowing most of the pieces listed above. Use the procedure checklist as a tool to know *your own* system. As a principal, I required each grade level to fill out the procedures checklist for their grade level. I kept it in a file and referenced it. If I found that staff members were not following it, then I had a meeting with them to determine what was happening.

2 THE LARGER SYSTEM—YOUR EXPECTATIONS AT THE CAMPUS LEVEL AND THE DISTRICT LEVEL

Once you know the systems being used in the classroom, the principal can articulate for the teachers the larger system. To continue the highway analogy, what happens if people repeatedly speed when they drive? They are taken out of the highway system and addressed by the much larger law enforcement/legal/judicial system. Sometimes students need to be taken out of the classroom system and addressed by the administration. So what are the components of the larger system?

1. The principal and/or assistant principal
2. The support staff (counselors, social workers, nurses, et al.)
3. Backup system of consequences and rewards (detention, school-sponsored parties, etc.)
4. District support system (alternative schools, student advocates, etc.)
5. Policies about suspension, expulsion, etc.

Many beginning teachers—just like beginning drivers—concentrate so much on their own performance and seldom consider the larger frames in which they are performing. As a principal, I answered the following questions for my staff and parents. I conducted a meeting with the students as well and explained what happened to them if they were exited from the classroom.

1. What is the principal's approach to discipline?
2. Who are the support staff persons available, and what are their roles?

3. What larger backup systems are available to individual teachers? For example: school-sponsored detention, Saturday school, timeout room, etc.
4. Does the district have a backup system for removing students from the school?
5. For which behaviors are students suspended? Expelled?

3 INDIVIDUAL STUDENTS

Ninety percent of your discipline referrals will come from 10% of your students. Skilled teachers and administrators identify these students within the first week of school. Students take on roles that determine many interactions within the classroom. To be sure, students can and do change, but certain behavioral patterns tend to emerge nonetheless. (See following chart with roles in the classroom.) These roles give each class a "personality." Some classes are much easier than others. Once skilled teachers identify the roles that students are playing in the classroom, they set up systems to help "manage" those roles. Sometimes a class will have a "critical mass" of difficult students. This will require an even more sophisticated and finely tuned systemic approach.

When there is a critical mass of difficult students in one room, the principal needs to intervene and move students to other classrooms or provide extra support for that one room.

In the highway analogy, what happens when the individual driver repeatedly endangers others? When there's a pattern of recklessness? When the individual drives drunk? How do you address individuals within the dynamics of the classroom?

Student Roles in the Classroom

TYPE	WANTS	INTERVENTIONS
Perfectionist	To be perfect	Make sure they have all the details. Provide a rubric for evaluation.
Bully	To be in control	Identify the parameters of behaviors acceptable in your classroom. This student will not respect you unless you are personally strong.
Silent	To be invisible	Call on the student. Set up academic tasks so the student must interact with someone.
Entertainer	To ease discomfort, provide fun	Provide opportunities with academic tasks for humor. Show the student you have a sense of humor about yourself.
Social connector	To be friends	Provide opportunity for him/her to talk while doing academic work.
Social isolate	* Varies by individual	Assign paired activities, which necessitate a social interaction. Outline the parameters of the behaviors of the classroom.
Arguer	To be right	Let the student have the last word but not the last 10 sentences. Build an opportunity to argue into academic tasks.
Leader	To take charge	Build opportunities for leadership into the classroom.
Instigator	To be in control	Clearly outline what will and will not be acceptable in your classroom. Have clear consequences. Build a relationship of mutual respect with this student.
Distracter	To not be held accountable academically	Identify the source of the problem. Can he/she read?
Special needs	* Varies by individual; may have biochemical or neurological basis	Identify the need.

Note. Ruby K. Payne, *A Framework for Understanding Poverty Trainer Certification Manual.*

4 INVOLVING PARENTS

Another piece of discipline puzzle is the role of students' parents/ guardians and your interactions with them. Should you involve them every time—or only some of the time? How do you determine when to involve them and to what extent? For what reasons?

To continue the highway analogy, what happens when the lawyers get involved and advocate for their client? Or what happens when the client does not have a lawyer? Who advocates for them? How does that change the dynamics? The same questions apply to students and their parents. To state it even more simply: When and how do you involve parents?

Basically, parents tend to fall into one of five groups:

- Overprotective
- Hands-off approach
- Concerned and appropriate
- Unavailable
- Caring but unable to help

So the approach you use will depend at least in part on the parent.

Parents have varying degrees of skills and understandings about students, children, and child development. It's important to note that most teachers and administrators have much more exposure to children and adolescents than most parents do. So the understandings that teachers and administrators have about student behaviors are often better developed and more research-based than many parents have. But most parents have a very deep emotional bond to the student (their child!) that the teacher doesn't have. Even if they don't "parent" their child as you wish they would, they love their children and will defend them.

How you approach parents will make a big difference. (See the following planning worksheet.) As an administrator, you can insist that this form be completed prior to the parent meeting or call—particularly for beginning teachers or experienced teachers who are going to have a difficult conference. Know what you want to accomplish before you have the phone conference or visit in person.

PARENT/TEACHER CONFERENCE FORM WITH STUDENT		
Student name	Date	Time
Parent name	Teacher	

PURPOSE OF CONFERENCE (CHECK AS MANY AS APPLY)
- [ ] scheduled teacher/parent conference
- [ ] student achievement issue
- [ ] parent-initiated
- [ ] discipline issue
- [ ] social/emotional issue

WHAT IS THE DESIRED GOAL OF THE CONFERENCE?

WHAT DATA WILL I OR THE STUDENT SHOW THE PARENT? Student work, discipline referrals, student planning documents?

WHAT QUESTIONS NEED TO BE ASKED? WHAT ISSUES NEED TO BE DISCUSSED?

WHAT FOLLOW-UP TOOLS AND STRATEGIES WILL BE IDENTIFIED?

Note. Ruby K. Payne, *Working with Parents: Building Relationships for Student Success,* 2nd ed., 2005, p. 51.

5 TEACHERS' APPROACH TO DISCIPLINE

Three basic beliefs about discipline tend to be used among teachers.

- Some believe that behavior is caused by the thinking and so use a more cognitive approach.
- Some believe behavior is developmental and so use a teaching/learning approach.
- Some believe behavior is strictly a learned response to prior stimuli.

Most teachers have a mix of beliefs and use a combined approach. In the research on styles of discipline, three are generally cited: authoritarian, permissive, and negotiated. Most skilled teachers use a combination—depending on the situation, the student, and the safety considerations.

The research on "voices" done by Eric Berne is particularly helpful. The voice the teacher starts out with usually determines the outcome of an incident. The *child* voice tends to be when a person is whining. The *parent* voice is a "telling" or "ordering" voice. There is a positive version (calm but insistent—example: "You must be seated now") and a negative version (when you have your index finger up and are giving a "should not" or "ought not to" lecture). The *adult* voice is when you're asking questions for understanding.

Research indicates that 80% of discipline referrals come from 11% of the teachers (which is the other side of the coin from the earlier-cited statistic that 90% of discipline referrals come from 10% of the students). One of the big reasons for the high number of referrals by a relatively small number of teachers is the tendency of many of those teachers to use the negative parent voice, which doesn't really help in changing student behavior.

The best approach is usually one in which the teacher starts out in the adult voice and finishes in the positive parent voice with a consequence. Examples:

- Adult voice—"Help me understand where you were for 25 minutes ..."
- Positive parent voice—"I'm sorry you chose to be lost for 25 minutes. Because of that choice, you also have chosen two hours in detention."

Most importantly, skilled teachers understand that when there is mutual respect in the classroom, discipline referrals drop. To quote Grant East, "Rules without relationships breed rebellion." For the classroom to be successful, there must be an atmosphere of mutual respect. The checklist for "Mutual Respect" can be used by the principal.

You, the principal, have the final responsibility for what happens on your campus just as the teacher is responsible for the classroom. For classrooms and campuses to work there has to be a final authority. That is you, the administrator. If that role is abdicated, the campus degenerates into chaos.

How do you build relationships of mutual respect?

Students look for—and need—three things:

- Insistence
- Support
- High expectations (not unreasonable, but high)

NAME:

1. What did you do? _____

2. When you did that, what did you want? _____

3. List four other things you could have done.

    1) _____

    2) _____

    3) _____

    4) _____

4. What will you do next time? _____

Rubric for Mutual Respect

Issue	Evidenced	Needed	Not Applicable
Teacher calls students by name.			
Teacher uses courtesies: "please," "thank you," etc.			
Students use courtesies with each other and with teacher.			
Teacher calls on all students.			
Teacher gets into proximity (within arm's reach) of all students—daily if possible, but at least weekly.			
Teacher greets students at door.			
Teacher smiles at students.			

Issue	Evidenced	Needed	Not Applicable
Classroom has businesslike atmosphere.			
Students are given tools to assess/ evaluate own work.			
Student-generated questions are used as part of instruction.			
Grading/scoring is clear and easily understood.			
Students may ask for extra help from teacher.			

Note. Ruby K. Payne, "Rubric for Mutual Respect," 2005.

6 ADDRESSING PARTICULAR INDIVIDUAL BEHAVIORS

Last, but not least, are the strategies for dealing with individual behaviors. Just as law enforcement has specific techniques for stopping a car, asking for a license, getting proof of insurance, etc., so you as the administrator need specific techniques for addressing particular behaviors.

Deciding if a particular behavior is actually a problem requires these questions:

1. Is this behavior endangering the student or other students?
2. Is this behavior interfering with teaching or learning?

If the answer to either of these questions is yes, then a discipline intervention needs to be identified and used.

Procedures Checklist

The following checklist is adapted from Guidelines for the First Days of School from the Research Development Center for Teacher Education, Research on Classrooms, University of Texas, Austin.

STARTING CLASS	MY PROCEDURE
Taking attendance	
Marking absences	
Tardy students	
Giving makeup work for absentees	
Enrolling new students	
Un-enrolling students	
Students who have to leave school early	
Warm-up activity (that students begin as soon as they walk into classroom)	

INSTRUCTIONAL TIME	MY PROCEDURE
Student movement within classroom	
Use of cell phones and headphones	
Student movement in and out of classroom	
Going to restroom	
Getting students' attention	
Students talking during class	
What students do when their work is completed	
Working together as group(s)	
Handing in papers/homework	
Appropriate headings for papers	

INSTRUCTIONAL TIME	MY PROCEDURE
Bringing/distributing/using textbooks	
Leaving room for special class	
Students who don't have paper and/or pencils	
Signal(s) for getting student attention	
Touching other students in classroom	
Eating food in classroom	
Laboratory procedures (materials and supplies, safety routines, cleaning up)	
Students who get sick during class	
Using pencil sharpener	
Listing assignments/homework/ due dates	
Systematically monitoring student learning during instruction	

ENDING CLASS	MY PROCEDURE
Putting things away	
Dismissing class	
Collecting papers and assignments	

OTHER	MY PROCEDURE
Lining up for lunch/recess/special events	
Walking to lunch/recess	
Putting away coats and backpacks	
Cleaning out locker	
Preparing for fire drills and/or bomb threats	
Going to gym for assemblies/pep rallies	
Respecting teacher's desk and storage areas	
Appropriately handling/using computers/ equipment	

STUDENT ACCOUNTABILITY	MY PROCEDURE
Late work	
Missing work	
Extra credit	
Redoing work and/or retaking tests	
Incomplete work	
Neatness	
Papers with no names	
Using pens, pencils, colored markers	
Using computer-generated products	
Internet access on computers	
Setting and assigning due dates	
Writing on back of paper	
Makeup work and amount of time for makeup work	

STUDENT ACCOUNTABILITY	MY PROCEDURE
Letting students know assignments missed during absence	
Percentage of grade for major tests, homework, etc.	
Explaining your grading policy	
Letting new students know your procedures	
Having contact with all students at least once during week	
Exchanging papers	
Using Internet for posting assignments and sending them in	

HOW WILL YOU ...	MY PLAN
Determine grades on report cards (components and weights of those components)?	
Grade daily assignments?	
Record grades so that assignments and dates are included?	
Have students keep records of their own grades?	
Make sure your assignments and grading reflect progress against standards?	
Notify parents when students are not passing or having other academic problems?	
Contact parents if problem arises regarding student behavior?	
Contact parents with positive feedback about their child?	
Keep records and documentation of student behavior?	
Document adherence to IEP (individualized education plan)?	
Return graded papers in timely manner?	
Monitor students who have serious health issues (peanut allergies, diabetes, epilepsy, etc.)?	

Toward a Cognitive Model for Better Understanding Socioeconomic Class

O NE OF THE PERSISTENT DEBATES in social-stratification research and theory pertains to the causation of both poverty and wealth. In fact, four prevalent theories are extant: individual choice, exploitation/colonialism, economic and social systems, and resources of a community. I would suggest a fifth explanation: the cognition and knowledge base of the individual and his/her relationships.

All disciplines move through three research stages: classification, correlation, and causation. For example, when people first saw the stars, they named them and called it astrology. Then Galileo came along and said the stars moved in relationship to each other and called that astronomy. And then Newton appeared and said there is a reason they do that and called it gravity. In social theory, however, there is no clear agreement about what causes social class.

Most legislation in the United States the last 70 years has been based on social determinism. In the 1800s, Western civilization tended to believe in genetic determinism. Who you were and what could happen to you were based largely on your genetic inheritance. Then the women's movement and the civil-rights movement came along and said it didn't matter what you were born with. If you aren't allowed to vote, own property, or be educated, then your genes were essentially a moot point. This is called social determinism. It's "the system" that holds you back. Beginning in the 1940s, we began to look at artificial intelligence, brain and MRI scans, and eventually computer programming. We became very interested in how individuals process and manipulate information and knowledge. It would seem it is time for a cognitive model of social class. In other words, what thinking and knowledge are necessary to function in different social-class environments? How can individual initiative—based on resources—overcome, even transcend, the very real impact of social determinism?

Social determinism is based on correlation models that use numbers as their main point of proof. In cognitive models of brain processing, the brain tends to process in patterns. As a person has greater expertise in a situation or discipline, he/she processes very rapidly in patterns (Gladwell, 2005; Bloom, 1976). So a cognitive model would rely more heavily on patterns of thinking as evidenced in patterns of behaviors. Many researchers are uncomfortable looking at patterns and would prefer the "safety" and proof of numbers. Yet experts in any discipline would agree that there are patterns of response among human beings.

Social determinism cannot answer the following questions:

- Why do only 42% of children born to parents in the bottom quintile stay in the bottom quintile? (Isaacs, 2007)
- Why do only 36% of the children born to households in the top quintile stay there?
- Why do 7% of individuals make it from the bottom 20% of household to the top 20% of households?
- Why are 75% of the Forbes list of the 400 wealthiest people in America new money?
- Why is there such a "great divide" in income by educational attainment?

And we know that there are correlates for poverty to the non-dominant race, to female gender, to disability, and to youth. However, if it were just about race, then whites wouldn't comprise 58% of the people in poverty in the United States (U.S. Census, 2000). And if poverty were just about female gender, then 75% of first-time prisoners wouldn't be uneducated males from poverty.

There must be additional causations. I will argue that there is a relationship between the demands of the environment, the resources one has, and the knowledge base one has.

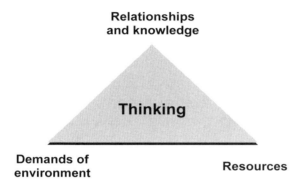

The Correlation Between Knowledge and What You Spend Your Time Doing

Knowledge is a huge form of privilege. How you spend your time determines to a large extent your knowledge base—and vice versa. In our research with individuals in poverty, this (see chart below) is what they say they spend their time on:

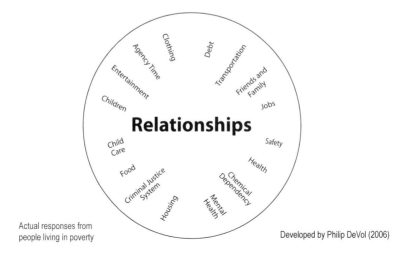

Actual responses from people living in poverty

Developed by Philip DeVol (2006)

This is what people in middle class (which we define as stability of resources—not just about money) say they spend their time on:

Developed by Philip DeVol (2006)

This is what people in wealth say they spend their time on:

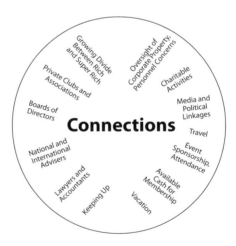

Developed by Ruby Payne (2005)

Just as social access, money, and being a member of the dominant group constitute forms of privilege, so is knowledge.

Resourced and Under-Resourced

Some individuals don't like the terminology of poverty, middle class, and wealth. Then let us use the terms resourced and under-resourced.

There are correlates that tend to occur as a person has fewer or greater resources.

UNDER-RESOURCED	. . . .	RESOURCED
Instability/crisis	. . . .	Stability
Isolation	. . . .	Exposure
Dysfunction	. . . .	Functionality
Concrete reality	. . . .	Abstract representational reality
Casual, oral language	. . . .	Written, formal register
Thought polarization	. . . .	Option seeking
Survival	. . . .	Abundance
No work/ intermittent work	. . . .	Work/careers/ larger cause
Poverty	. . . .	Wealth
Less educated	. . . .	More educated

Resources that bring stability include the following:

FINANCIAL
Having the money to purchase goods and services.

EMOTIONAL
Being able to choose and control emotional responses, particularly to negative situations, without engaging in self-destructive behavior. This is an internal resource and shows itself through stamina, perseverance, and choices.

MENTAL
Having the mental abilities and acquired skills (reading, writing, computing) to deal with daily life.

SPIRITUAL
Believing in divine purpose and guidance.

PHYSICAL
Having physical health and mobility.

SUPPORT SYSTEMS
Having friends, family, and backup resources available to access in times of need. These are external resources.

RELATIONSHIPS/ROLE MODELS
Having frequent access to adult(s) who are appropriate, who are *nurturing,* and who do not engage in self-destructive behavior.

KNOWLEDGE OF HIDDEN RULES
Knowing the unspoken cues and habits of a group.

LANGUAGE/FORMAL REGISTER
Having the vocabulary, language ability, and negotiation skills necessary to succeed in school and/or work settings.

Research Examples of the Frame of Environmental Demands, Relationships, and Knowledge

In a study after Hurricane Katrina hit New Orleans, it was found that the people in poverty who made it out of poor neighborhoods had more social capital than the people in poverty who didn't make it out.

Chicago researchers (Berliner et al., 2009) found that "neighborhood efficacy" or lack thereof did more to impact student achievement than the family did. So the "thinking" and the mindset of the environment are a huge factor in behavior.

We know from research in Australia (Najman et al., 2004) that the verbal comprehension scores of 5-year-olds and the non-verbal reasoning scores of 14-year-olds was significantly correlated to the maternal grandfather's occupation. So the combination of knowledge base and learning environment in a family system over the generations also plays a key role in the potential of young people.

Conclusion

For most of the last 70 years U.S. legislators have used a compliance model based on social determinism in an attempt to eradicate poverty. It simply hasn't worked. Isn't it time to consider additional causations and explanations? If you only give individuals resources but don't give them the capacity to develop those resources, then a government creates a group of individuals who *cannot* develop their own resource base. This is not a sustainable model. The role of knowledge in creating resources cannot be underestimated. It must be incorporated into a better understanding of class structures—and how they develop—in the United States.

References

Berliner, D. C. (2009). *Poverty and potential: Out-of-school factors and school success.* Boulder: National Educational Policy Center. Retrieved from http://epicpolicy.org/publication/poverty-and-potential

Bloom, B. (1976). *Human characteristics and school learning.* New York, NY: McGraw-Hill.

Forbes 400 richest Americans. (2011). New York, NY: Forbes.com LLC. Retrieved from http://www.forbes.com/wealth/forbes-400

Gladwell, M. (2005). *Blink: The power of thinking without thinking.* New York, NY: Little, Brown.

Isaacs, J. B. (2007). Economic mobility across generations. Economic Mobility Project, Pew Charitable Trusts. Retrieved from http://www.pewtrusts.org/uploadedFiles/wwwpewtrustsorg/Reports/Economic_Mobility/EMP%20Across%20Generations%20ES%20+%20Chapter.pdf

Najman, J. M., Aird, R., Bor, W., O'Callaghan, M., Williams, G. M., & Shuttlewood, G. J. (2004). The generational transmission of socioeconomic inequalities in child cognitive development and emotional health. *Social Science and Medicine, 58*(6), 1147–1158. doi:10.1016/S0277-9536(03)00286-7

U.S. Bureau of the Census. (2000). www.census.gov

Where Do We Go from Here? How Do Communities Develop Intellectual Capital and Sustainability?

A KEY DISCUSSION IN THE UNITED STATES in the new millennium centers on community. Urban areas have not had a good model for community. Rural areas are losing population and the sense of community they have always had. In fact, the only community that many rural areas have anymore is the local school district. As the student count shrinks and conversations about consolidation begin, many communities vigorously resist that effort because intuitively they understand the need for community.

For the purposes of this article, the definition of community will be the one used by Carl Taylor and Daniel Taylor-Ide in the book *Just and Lasting Change: When Communities Own Their Futures.* They write: "Community, as we use the term, is any group that has something in common and the potential for acting together" (p. 19).

Taylor and Taylor-Ide have been involved with community development for many years around the world. *"The key to building better lives,"* they state, *"is not technical breakthroughs but changing behavior at the community level ... in ways that fit local circumstances.* ... Playing an essential role in these processes are the formation and maintenance of a genuine three-way partnership among people in the community, experts from the outside, and government officials" (pp. 17–18).

Community development is becoming more imperative because of the relationship between the intellectual capital in the community and its economic well-being.

What is intellectual capital?

Thomas Stewart, in his book *Intellectual Capital: The New Wealth of Organizations,* defines it as the "intangible assets—the talents of its people, the efficacy of its management systems, the character of its relationships to its customers ..." It is the ability to take existing information and turn it into useful knowledge and tools.

Intellectual capital has become the economic currency of the 21st century. In the 1900s the economic currency was industry-based. In the 1800s it was agriculture-based. One of the issues for many communities is the loss of jobs related to industry and agriculture. Wealth creation is now linked to intellectual capital.

What is the relationship between economic well-being and the development of capital?

Right now in the world and in the United States there is a direct correlation between the level of educational attainment in a community or country and its economic wealth. In the book *As the Future Catches You,* Juan Enriquez gives the following statistic: In 1980 the differential between the richest and poorest country in the world was 5:1 as measured by GNP. In 2001 the differential between the richest and the poorest country in the world was 390:1 as measured by gross national product. GNP is directly linked to the level of educational attainment. So growth is not incremental; it is exponential.

For the future well-being of communities, it becomes necessary to begin the serious and deliberate development of intellectual capital. This is easier said than done.

How do communities develop intellectual capital? How do you translate between the poor and the policymakers/powerbrokers?

Systems tend to operate out of default and are amoral. Systems are only as moral as the people who are in them. One of the big issues is how different economic groups translate the issues. For a group to work together, there must be a shared understanding and vocabulary. What is a huge issue to an individual in poverty often doesn't translate as an issue in wealth. The policymakers/powerbrokers tend to be at the wealth level, while the bureaucrats are at the middle-class level. In the book *Seeing Systems*, Barry Oshry talks about the difficulty the three levels have in communicating with each other.

The chart identifies how issues are addressed at different economic levels.

POVERTY	MIDDLE CLASS	WEALTH
Having a job Hourly wages	Appropriate, challenging job Salary and benefits	Maintenance and growth of assets Quality and quantity of workforce
Safety of schools	Quality of schools	K–12 higher education continuum Technical innovation Intermediate colleges and trade schools
A place to rent/live Affordable housing	Property values Quality of schools Quality of neighborhood	Corporate investment potential Infrastructure to support development
Welfare benefits	Taxes	Balance of trade Percentage of taxes Tort liability Corporate contributions Percentage of government indebtedness

continued on next page

continued from previous page

POVERTY	MIDDLE CLASS	WEALTH
Fairness of law enforcement Gangs	Safety Crime rates	Risk management Bond ratings Insurance ratings
Access to emergency rooms	Cost of medical insurance Quality and expertise of medical profession	Cost/predicted costs of medical benefits Workers' compensation
Public transportation	Network of freeways Traffic congestion Time commuting	Systems of transportation (railway, bus, air, etc.) Maintenance of the infrastructure
Have enough food	Access to quality restaurants Variety/quality of food available	Access to high-quality restaurants Amenities for clients Availability of fresh food

As you can see, the same issue is approached and viewed very differently, depending on the economic level of the individual.

What would be the advantage to a community to translate between and among levels for a shared understanding?

With shared understandings, one can develop community, create economic well-being, and develop sustainability.

What is sustainability?

Many people believe that the first major revolution in the world was the agricultural revolution when people were not moving but "stayed put" and had time to develop crafts and skills—and devote time to learning. Many also believe that the second major revolution was the industrial revolution when tools were used to spur development. Finally, the third major revolution may well be the development of sustainability. In other words, how do we use our resources, yet have enough available for the next generation? How do we live in our environment, yet maintain it for our children?

The following index lists major areas of sustainability.

SUSTAINABLE DEVELOPMENT INDEX (SDI)

1. Human rights, freedom, quality	A. Politics and human rights B. Equality
2. Demographic development and life expectancy	C. Demographic development D. Life expectancy, mortality
3. State of health and healthcare	E. Healthcare F. Disease and nutrition
4. Education	G. Education H. Technologies and information sharing
5. Economic development and foreign indebtedness	I. Economy J. Indebtedness
6. Resource consumption, eco-efficiency	K. Economy—genuine savings L. Economy—resource consumption
7. Environmental quality, environmental pollution	M. Environment—natural resources, land use N. Environment—urban and rural problems

Note. This is the Sustainable Development Index (SDI) developed in 2000-01 by the Central European Node of the Millennium Project through the American Council for the United Nations University. In 1987 the World Commission on Environment and Development defined sustainability as a concept. In 1992 a total of 178 states agreed at the United Nations Conference of Environment and Development to include this concept in official development measures. Consensus appears to be emerging that sustainable development may well be "the third global revolution," following the agricultural and industrial revolutions (Mederly, Novacek, Topercer, pp. 5, 8).

It is from the first four elements (above) that intellectual capital is developed. Those four are foundational to the development of all others.

Why must equity precede sustainability?

One of the most interesting dynamics in communities is the impact of critical mass and equity on change. Thomas Sowell, a historical and international demographer, states that if a community allows any group to be disenfranchised for any reason (religion, race, class, etc.), the whole community becomes economically poorer. What happens is as follows:

10%	20%	30%	40%	50%	60%	70%	80%	90%	(top 10%)

Let's use poverty as an example. When 10% of a community is poor, most members of the community will say they have no poverty. When the number climbs to 20%, most will say there is very little poverty. When the number climbs to 30%, the comment will be that there are a few individuals in poverty in the community. But when it hits 35% to 40%, the community becomes alarmed. (Thirty-five percent to 40% is typically the point of critical mass. Critical mass is when enough people are involved that the issue/behavior gets above the radar screen and the community notices.) Comments are made that, all of a sudden, all these poor people came!

At that point in time, the top 10% of the community, which has most of the money and resources, will typically pass laws and ordinances to control the 40%. In the United States now the top 10% of households (as measured by income) pays 70% of all federal taxes. The bottom 50% of households pay 4% of federal taxes. By the time the poor population reaches 60% to 70% of the total community population, the top 10% of households will move out, leaving the community with very few resources. The community is no longer sustainable.

What process can communities use to develop both intellectual capital and sustainability?

To foster community involvement, it's important to use processes that are relatively simple and involve a large number of people, so that critical mass can be achieved. This process must be at least a 20- to 25-year plan, because it takes that long to get critical mass. As Paul Saffo, director of the Institute for the Future, states, "It takes 20 years to become an overnight success" (*BusinessWeek,* August 25, 2003).

It is my recommendation that communities secure endowments. What the endowment does is ensure that for 25 years the ensuing process is followed, data are collected, and three groups are always involved: people in the community, outside experts, and government officials.

The process I recommend takes a minimum of 20 years and follows these steps:

Step 1
A community group gets together. The members of the group identify what their ideal community would be like 20 years hence. They identify six or seven issues (using the sustainability index as a guide) that would most enhance their community.

Step 2
The group identifies the key markers for each issue that would indicate progress toward that ideal.

Step 3
The group identifies the current status of those indicators by gathering "real" community data.

Step 4
The group works backward and identifies what the marker would look like 18 years from the goal, 16 years from the goal, etc. Measurements for the markers are established.

Step 5

The group goes to the larger community (including government officials) and asks all agencies, foundations, charities, churches, businesses, etc., which if any of the markers they are currently working on or would be willing to help address. The larger community agrees to gather data and report that data once a year.

Step 6

The individuals overseeing the endowment gather the data, put it into a report and, once a year, gather all the larger community for a breakfast and report the data. The leadership persons make suggested recommendations for external expert assistance. The larger community recommits for another year to the larger goals and collection of data.

Step 6 is repeated every year

It will take 10 to 12 years before much progress at all is seen. Then the progress will become noticeable. Within 20 years the progress will be dramatic.

Why use this process?

In the history of community development, one of four approaches tends to be used: blueprint, explosion, additive, or biological (Taylor & Taylor-Ide). The biological approach is one of tensegrity. "Tensegrity is the biological form of building," say the authors. "It works by balancing systems in flexible homeostasis rather than by building in a mechanical way that attaches its components rigidly" (p. 58). According to Taylor and Taylor-Ide, tensegrity has these characteristics:

- It allows forms to move and reshape.
- It uses self-assembly in locally specific patterns.
- The whole is different from the member parts.
- It has information feedback.
- It has an efficient distribution and redistribution system.
- It brings accountability; when one part is irresponsible, the whole system is out of balance.

What can you do to get individuals from poverty involved in community issues?

1. Understand the nature of systems. What appeals to the decision makers and power brokers doesn't have the same appeal in poverty and vice versa.
2. Work on real issues—issues that impact day-to-day life.
3. Approach the poor as problem solvers, not victims.
4. Teach the adult voice.
5. Teach question making.
6. Teach "backward" planning ("begin with the end in mind").
7. Start the process by building relationships of mutual respect, using videos, food, and entertainment; identify the power brokers in the poor community (corner grocers, hairdressers, barbers, ministers, et al.) and bring them into the process.
8. Pay them for their time (e.g., with inexpensive gift cards).
9. Let them bring their children.
10. Identify common tasks so that conversation can occur.
11. Provide constructive outlets for frustration and criticism.
12. Use mental models to help identify, with a minimum of emotion, the areas of needed change.
13. *Gather real data.*

Why would a community consider such an endowed process?

Quoting Taylor and Taylor-Ide,

> For rich and poor alike, the expansion of trade, changes in the Earth's environment, and the unraveling of social systems make the future uncertain. Even wealthy societies are increasingly unable to care for their growing numbers of poor, alienated youth, forgotten elderly, marginalized mothers, hostile homeless, and exploited minorities ... To achieve a more just and lasting future, we must continually update our definition of development. We can advance more confidently and effectively into that unknown territory by drawing lessons from past successes—and from past failures—and by tailoring solutions for each community to its specific hopes, capabilities, and resources. (p. 30)

In short, community development—based on intellectual capital—is not really a choice. Our sustainability, even survival, depends on it.

References

Enriquez, Juan. (2001). *As the future catches you*. New York, NY: Crown Business.

Oshry, Barry. (1995). *Seeing systems: Unlocking the mysteries of organizational life*. San Francisco, CA: Berrett-Koehler Publishers.

Saffo, Paul. (2003, August). Speaking out: Institute for the Future's Paul Saffo. *BusinessWeek*.

Sowell, Thomas. (1998, October 5). Race, culture and equality. *Forbes*.

Sowell, Thomas. (1997). *Migrations and cultures: A world view*. New York, NY: HarperCollins.

Stewart, Thomas A. (1997). *Intellectual capital: The new wealth of organizations*. New York, NY: HarperCollins.

Taylor, Carl, & Taylor-Ide, Daniel. (2002.) *Just and lasting change: When communities own their futures*. Baltimore, MD: Johns Hopkins University Press.

Moving from Middle Class to Situational Poverty—from Stability to Instability: What You Can Do to Help Your Students and Parents During the Present Economic Downturn

First published in *Instructional Leader,* May 2009.
Reprinted with permission. *Instructional Leader* is produced by the
Texas Elementary Principals and Supervisors Association. © 2012.

B ECAUSE OF THE CURRENT RECESSION, many principals and teachers are reporting to me the growing number of students and parents who are seeking assistance through the school, as well as increasing numbers of students who are homeless. There is a great reluctance on the part of people who have been in the middle class to admit that their resource base is becoming unstable. In my book *A Framework for Understanding Poverty* (1996, 2005), the continuum from poverty to wealth is defined as "the extent to which you have resources."

RESOURCES

FINANCIAL
Having the money to purchase goods and services.

LANGUAGE
Being able to speak and use formal register in writing and in speech.

EMOTIONAL
Being able to choose and control emotional responses, particularly to negative situations, without engaging in self-destructive behavior. This is an internal resource and shows itself through stamina, perseverance, and choices.

continued on next page

continued from previous page

MENTAL
Having the mental abilities and acquired skills (reading, writing, computing) to deal with daily life.

SPIRITUAL
Believing in divine purpose and guidance.

PHYSICAL
Having physical health and mobility.

SUPPORT SYSTEMS
Having friends, family, and backup resources available to access in times of need. These are external resources.

RELATIONSHIPS/ROLE MODELS
Having frequent access to adult(s) who are appropriate, who are nurturing to the child, and who do not engage in self-destructive behavior.

KNOWLEDGE OF HIDDEN RULES
Knowing the unspoken cues and habits of a group.

Note. Ruby K. Payne, adapted and reprinted with permission from *A Framework for Understanding Poverty,* 1996, 2005.

The first thing that happens in a severe economic downturn is that hope and choice are replaced with fear and a sense of scarcity. When fear and scarcity come into one's thinking, the brain is less able to seek options or see possibilities. The negative "parent voice" takes over the internal conversation with the self. For adults who have never experienced unemployment, insufficient funds to pay the mortgage, or the need to sell things for cash, there's considerable confusion because the knowledge base isn't available to know what the choices are. Furthermore, in middle class it's usually seen as a personal failing to lose a job or not be able to pay the mortgage. So it often isn't shared right away. Making things worse, credit cards often are used as a short-term borrowing mechanism to avoid the possibility of losing one's house, which then exacerbates the financial issues.

As adults begin to assess the reality of their situation, most go through the five stages of grief as outlined by Kübler-Ross. These five stages are denial, anger, bargaining, depression, acceptance. A person tends to move back and forth along this continuum. Middle class generally makes its decisions about time and money against these three factors: work, achievement, and material security. When you have lost your job, you have lost two of the three decision makers—work and material security. It then impacts your identity: Who are you if you don't have work? If you cannot keep your house? If your material security is breached? Then how do you make decisions? Furthermore, the two rules about money that middle class uses are now out the window: (1) "I don't ask you for money, and you don't ask me" and (2) "If you borrow money, you have to pay it back." Personal pride and the deeply ingrained hidden rules about money are now challenged. Furthermore, it's typically taboo in middle class to tell people that you're in financial trouble. Middle class has another hidden rule about personal money, and it's simply that you don't talk about it. So asking a middle-class person to participate in a group sharing session about finances usually isn't going to happen—particularly for the men because male identity in middle class is, first and foremost, about being a provider.

The adults then are moving through the stages of grief as the resource base becomes less predictable and stable. For example, as the financial resources disappear, the emotional resources become less predictable. The spiritual resources of hope and optimism tend to be replaced with fear and scarcity. Relationships become strained. Support systems either are not accessed or become thin. And the hidden rules don't work anymore for this new situation. Life becomes about day-to-day survival. More time is spent accessing fewer resources—i.e., food, shelter, money.

And you lose social capital. You find out in a hurry who your real friends are. You say things that are less than fully accurate. For example, when money is tight, you don't go out to eat as part of a social group. You say things like, "I need to help my daughter with her homework" or "That evening doesn't work for us." In time, the very individuals who could provide support are not available. *And,* when they find out you've lost your job, there's reluctance on their part to ask you to join the group because no one wants to embarrass you. So the support systems become thinner.

Three times in my marriage of 31 years, my former husband lost his job because of recessions. I can tell you from personal experience that it's not only financially difficult but emotionally devastating. It impacts identity, self-worth, and personal value. The stages of grief are so palpable that you can touch them on a daily basis. Furthermore, the resource base that you worked so hard to develop erodes before your eyes—much faster than it took to develop it. Even if the words are there, you can't talk about it every day. Anxiety is the cousin of fear. Anxiety produces cortisol, which makes anxiety increase. So less is said every day, and certain topics are avoided. Eventually, each person goes to his or her own corner to worry, to work through the fears—*alone.*

This in turn impacts children. Often middle-class parents don't want to burden their children with fear or don't tell the children. But the child usually knows when things aren't right. And so students may become withdrawn, act out, or involve themselves in substance abuse.

How does the school help students deal with the grieving and the shift in resources?

1. Journal writing: Give students questions or topics to write about. For example: What do you think it feels like to lose a job? Should the government give money and provide support for those who have lost their homes? How does it feel when you can't have many of the same things your friends have? Which is more important—things or love? Why?

2. Have teachers look for "red flag" behaviors:
   □ Truancy
   □ Patterns of tardiness
   □ "Acting out" or withdrawn behaviors

- ☐ Knowledge of, or conversation about, sex and drugs inappropriate for the child's age or stage of development
- ☐ Delays in common adaptive-behavior skills
- ☐ Lower-than-expected academic performance
- ☐ Inability to build or maintain appropriate peer and/or adult relationships
- ☐ Anxiety, fearfulness, flinching
- ☐ Inability to cope with transitions during the school day
- ☐ Lethargy, sleeping at school
- ☐ Hunger
- ☐ Poor hygiene
- ☐ Encopresis, enuresis, or other unusual toileting habits
- ☐ Unusual eating habits or patterns
- ☐ Somatic complaints
- ☐ Lack of parental interest in child's basic health or school performance

Note. Heatherly W. Conway, *Collaboration For Kids,* 2006, p. 19.

Refer to the counselor or office if these behaviors show up. Provide coping strategies and access to community resources.

3. All of us orient ourselves to daily life through space, time, and ritual. For example, I get up in the morning at 5 a.m., use the bathroom, make coffee, go online, and check my e-mails. All of these things involve space, time, and ritual. When you're homeless, all of these are disrupted. You don't know where your things are, routines are not predictable—nor is time. There are other people in the bathroom, you cannot go to the computer, you only have a few things ... what you can carry with you. So for students who are homeless, provide them with a place in the classroom that is *their own space* to put their things where they can find them. Allow them to keep a couple of extra things there if they aren't dangerous, such as mementos, stickers, etc.). Give them a morning routine when they come into the class—i.e., "Do these three things first." Routine calms and orients people.

How does the school help parents deal with the grieving and the shift in resources?

1. Encourage parents to talk to their children about their personal economic situation. Assure the children that it won't last forever. Provide an analogy for children to help them understand. For example, remember when you were riding your bicycle and you had to pedal hard to get up the hill, and you stopped and took a rest to get to the top, and then you got to coast down the hill? Well, right now we're riding the bicycle up the money hill, and we're having to stop and take a rest. So we aren't going to buy this or this or this; those will come later when we're coasting *down* the hill.

2. Put the situation in a long-term perspective. Ask these questions: Will this situation last forever? *No.* Have I lost the people I love? *No.* What am I learning from this situation that will help me in the future? How has this situation changed my thinking?

3. In the research, if you are homeless, religious social capital does more to move you out of being homeless than any other form of assistance. Link the homeless family with a church, synagogue, mosque, or other religious organization.

4. Pair men together (not groups): "A father came in yesterday about the same situation ... Would you be willing to talk to him?"

5. Provide a list of linkages where food and other forms of assistance are available.

6. Share this article with parents. This may be their situation or that of their siblings or their neighbors. When people understand that they aren't going through this alone, there is more ability to name the experience and deal with it.

7. Develop a plan to address the current situation (sometimes termed situational poverty), along with a future story that includes what you will do when this situation is past.

8. Provide a list of books that you have read or staff has read that talk about what it's like to go through tough times. This could include autobiographies/biographies of individuals who have gone through very difficult times—for example, Lincoln or Einstein or Michelangelo. Sometimes someone else's story puts our own in perspective: "I cried because I had no shoes until I met a man who had no feet."

9. *Do not engage in pity.* That is humiliating for the persons receiving it. If they have the courage to tell you about their situation, accept it, and give them time to talk about their thoughts and feelings. Focus the conversation on what they will do next. Having a plan usually helps with anxiety.

Conclusion

It isn't the school's responsibility to provide resources for students and parents in this time of economic downturn. It is, however, the school's responsibility to provide high expectations, insistence, and support for students academically and behaviorally. To do that, some understanding of the students' personal situation needs to be acknowledged. All learning is double-coded—both emotionally and cognitively.

When I was principal of an elementary school, a sixth-grader was determined to come to school the morning after his father was killed in an auto accident at 2 am. A neighbor brought the boy to school and the neighbor said to me, "I don't understand why he insisted on coming to school." I said to the neighbor, "I do. It's the one place in his life that is still the same, that is predictable and he knows what is going to happen. There's a routine. The rest of his life is up for grabs. He needed to know that one place in his life is stable." I took the boy into my office and said to him, "I can't bring your life before your father died back for you. But I can help you cope. Go on to class. If you need to leave, tell your teacher to let you come back to the office— and then you and I can figure out how to handle the rest of your day."

Education can give you the language, the tools, and the options to move beyond a situation. That is a gift we can give to our children and. sometimes, their parents. Schools can be a tremendous source of stability and routine for children, even when their own world seems to be falling apart.

References

Conway, Heatherly W. (2006). *Collaboration for kids: Early-intervention tools for schools and communities.* Highlands, TX: aha! Process.

Greenspan, Stanley I., & Benderly, Beryl L. (1998). *The growth of the mind and the endangered origins of intelligence.* Cambridge, MA: Da Capo Press.

Kübler-Ross, Elisabeth. (1969). *On death and dying.* New York, NY: Macmillan Publishing.

Payne, Ruby K. (1996, 2005). *A framework for understanding poverty* (5th ed.). Highlands, TX: aha! Process.

Payne, Ruby K. (2008). *Under-resourced learners: 8 strategies to boost student achievement.* Highlands, TX: aha! Process.

Impacting Two Generations at Once: Refocusing Parent Training to Develop Human Capacity and Community Sustainability

with Philip E. DeVol

First published (excerpt) in *Instructional Leader,* July 2009. Reprinted with permission. *Instructional Leader* is produced by the Texas Elementary Principals and Supervisors Association. © 2012.

A LWAYS THE DEBATE IN SCHOOLS is what to do about parent training and involvement. Title I requires parent training and involvement.

Intergenerational Transfer of Knowledge

Increasingly research is looking at the intergenerational transfer of knowledge. A study done in Australia—which followed the children of 8,556 women (mostly from poverty) from their first clinic visit for pregnancy, again at age 5, and again at age 14 (Najman et al., 2004)—found that the child's maternal grandfather's occupational status independently predicted the child's verbal comprehension levels at age 5 and the non-verbal reasoning scores at age 14.

Why would the maternal grandfather's *occupation* be so predictive? The occupation would tell you the level of stability in the household and be a predictor of the level of education. Because the mother is so instrumental in the early nurturing of the child and the vocabulary the child hears, it would follow that the mother's access to knowledge and vocabulary would be based on her own childhood experiences. Therefore, the maternal grandfather's occupation would be instrumental in predicting achievement. The Hart and Risley study

(1995) found that a 3-year-old in a professional household has more vocabulary than an adult in a welfare household.

It would be very easy for educators to now dismiss attempts to educate children by saying it all depends on what their grandfather did. But someone taught the grandfather, and someone taught the mother. Therefore, current educators can impact two generations through the students they have in their classrooms and changing the focus of parent training.

Impact of Poverty on Brain Functioning

The key issues here are language acquisition and the development of the prefrontal/executive functions of the brain.

Researchers at the University of California, Berkeley did research using electroencephalography (EEG) to compare the brains of poor children with those of middle class children. The subjects ranged in age from 7 to 12. Mark Kishiyama, lead researcher, indicated that the patterns in poor children's brains were very similar to adults who have had strokes and therefore have lesions in their prefrontal cortex. The prefrontal cortex (executive function) controls working memory, behavioral self-regulation, cognitive control, reward processing, and problem-solving ability. "There are a number of factors associated with LSES rearing conditions that may have contributed to these results such as greater levels of stress and lack of access to cognitively stimulating materials and experiences" (Kishiyama, Boyce, Jimenez, Perry, & Knight, in press, p. 1). It follows that if the parent came from poverty, the executive functions would not be as well developed so they could not be passed on to the children. You cannot teach what you do not know.

Impact of Poverty on Individuals and Organizations

What we know about poverty is that its instability forces people into the tyranny of the moment. It requires that people must be able to use their reactive skills to solve immediate concrete problems. The more a person's attention is drawn to the present moment, the harder it is to maintain a future orientation. It follows that it's also harder then for kids to concentrate on achievement. In fact, Cornell University did research with poor children and found that the more stressful the environment, the less effective working memory/executive function was (Schamberg, 2008).

When times get tough and money runs short, organizations tend to focus down on their core mission, limit extraneous activities, and tighten the grip on the budget to ensure the organization's immediate survival. Like individuals impacted by poverty, an organization spends time and energy solving the same old problems over and over. In essence the organization has moved from an abstract world to a concrete world.

In the work we do with adults in poverty, the first rule for making the transition out of poverty is to think about the future, to think abstractly, even when you are living in the midst of concrete problems. That should be the first rule for organizations too. To do that, you have to develop and use executive functions, as well as language.

Impact of Education Across Generations and Sustainable Communities

What we know as educators is that we have a tremendous amount of influence on the lives of children and their parents. We also know that if children in the K–6 years have language experience, brain development, and cognitive learning structures, then they will be more successful through Grade 12. Miller and DeVol (2009) have created a continuum [link to continuum http://ahaprocess.com/files/Bridges_Continuum.pdf] that shows the importance of education upon the entire community. When we successfully educate and graduate our students, we as educators have a huge impact on job retention, careers, post-secondary success, wellness, and community prosperity.

Why the emphasis on a sustainable community? As communities lose their resources, their ability to develop future resources—i.e., employment, education of children, care for natural resources, be-

THE BRIDGES CONTINUUM
COMPREHENSIVE STRATEGIES FOR BRIDGES STEERING COMMITTEES

	Birth to 6	K–12	Post-Secondary	Workforce Prep/Placement
Metrics: Ending Poverty Scorecard	Ready for school Language experience, brain development, cognitive learning structures	Graduation rates GEDs	Retention rates Graduation rates Certifications	Employment rate Apprenticeships Certifications Availability of jobs Mix of jobs
Fallout Costs	Failure to act here means giving up the highest returns on dollars spent on interventions; for birth to 5 the returns can be as high as 15–17%. [i]	Dropouts from the class of 2007 will cost the U.S. nearly $329 billion in lost wages, taxes, and productivity in their lifetimes. [ii]	Loss of income: lifetime earnings of a male with a bachelor's degree in 2004 were 96% higher than a male with a high school diploma. [iii]	Young men with low earnings and employment rates are much more likely than others to engage in crime, less likely to marry, and more likely to father children outside of marriage. Crime imposes costs of as much as $1–2 trillion per year. The savings that can be realized by preventing crime and delinquency among youth are extremely high. [iv]
Family of Strategies Using aha! Process Constructs	*Tucker Signing Strategies* *Reading by Age 5* Getting Ahead® Develop an early-childhood champion *Until It's Gone/ Circles®*	Ruby Payne schools— *Framework* training *The R Rules* *Collaboration For Kids* Dropout prevention Financial literacy *Until It's Gone/ Circles*	*Helping Under-Resourced Learners Succeed at the College and University Level.* (for administrators) *Investigations into Economic Class in America* *Understanding and Engaging Under-Resourced College Students* (for faculty and instructors) *Until It's Gone/Circles* targeting barriers and academic performance	Cascade Engineering/ Quest Cincinnati Works The Source Getting Ahead *Until It's Gone/Circles* to support placement and barrier removal
Who Takes Responsibility for Change	Families, early-childhood development field	Parents, students, educators, school boards, PTAs, taxpayers	Students, faculty, administrators, boards, communities, benefactors	Employers, employees, government, colleges, chambers of commerce, economic and community developers, workforce development, high school

[i] Heckman, James J. "Investing in Disadvantaged Young Children is an Economically Efficient Policy." Paper presented at Committee for Economic Development, the Pew Charitable Trusts, PNC Financial Services Group Forum on "Building the Economic Case for Investments in Preschool." New York, January 10, 2006.
[ii] High School Dropouts in America, Alliance for Excellent Education, http://www.all4ed.org/files/GraduationRates_FactSheet.pdf
[iii] Kirsch, Irwin, Braun, Henry, Yamamoto, Kentaro. (January 2007). "America's Perfect Storm: Three Forces Changing Our Nation's Future." Princeton, NJ: Educational Testing Service.
[iv] Holzer, Harry J. "Workforce Development and the Disadvantaged." The Urban Institute, Brief 7, September 2008. www.urban.org/UploadPDF/411761_workforce_development.PDF

Prepared by Scott Miller of Move the Mountain, Inc. and Philip DeVol of aha! Process, Inc.

www.ahaprocess.com
www.movethemountain.org
© 2009 by aha! Process, Inc.
© 2009 Move the Mountain

Job Retention	Self-Sufficient Income	Seniors	Wellness	Community Prosperity
One-year minimum	Self-sufficient wage (Wider Opportunities for Women) 200% poverty guidelines goals met for households Assets established	Poverty rate Access to housing and healthcare	High resources—all 11 Balanced life Giving back to the community	Environmental sustainability Economic viability where everyone can live well Low rates of poverty and disparity Social Health Indices are positive
$5,505.08 average turnover cost for an $8.00 an hour employee [v]	Children who live in families with an annual income less than $15,000 are 22 times more likely to be abused or neglected than children living in families with an annual income of $30,000 or more. [vi]	Individuals 55 and older accounted for 22% of all personal bankruptcies in 2007, compared with 8% in 1991. Healthcare costs proved to be the top reason for many of these bankruptcies. [vii]	Poor rankings in the OECD (Organization for Economic Co-operation and Development) [viii]	Persistent childhood poverty is estimated to cost our nation $500 billion a year, or about 4% of GDP. [ix] Communities that have lost manufacturing jobs, businesses, and their tax base are not viable economically and socially.
Cascade Engineering/ Quest Cincinnati Works The Source Getting Ahead for new employees *Until It's Gone/* Circles Working Bridges Employer Workgroup, Vermont	Employer in-house advancement strategies Bridges training Getting Ahead Cascade Engineering/ Quest Cincinnati Works The Source *Until It's Gone*/Circles for advancement	Wider Opportunities for Women *Until It's Gone/* Circles	Sophisticated service delivery systems— consulting Community Collaboration, Inc., Northern Illinois University *Until It's Gone* community engagement models, Circles Campaign Champions by discipline *Tactical Communication*	Bridges Steering Committees Community Sustainability Grid Systemic change and policy issues addressed by all sectors *Until It's Gone*/Circles
Employers, employees, chambers of commerce, economic and community developers, workforce development, human services, government	Policymakers, employers, employees, workforce development, government, human services	Service providers, faith community, government, neighborhood associations, civic groups	Faith community, civic organizations, medical community, law enforcement, neighborhood associations, political parties	Bridges Steering Committees, people and organizations from all other points on the continuum. People from all classes, races, and political persuasions

Compilation of Turnover Studies, SASHA Corporation, http://www.sashacorp.com/turnframe.html
American Humane, http://www.americanhumane.org/about-us/newsroom/fact-sheets/americas-children.html
Health Care Costs, Economy Pushing Senior Citizens to Bankruptcy and Poverty in the U.S., Senior Journal.com. http://seniorjournal.com/NEWS/
SeniorStats/2008/20080826-USSeniorCitizensInPoverty.htm
Burd-Sharps, Sarah, et al. (2008) The Measure of America: American Human Development Report 2008-2009. New York, NY: Columbia University Press.
Center for American Progress, From Poverty to Prosperity: A National Strategy to Cut Poverty in Half, April 2007. www.americanprogress.org/issues/2007/04/pdf/
poverty_report.pdf.

ing healthy, etc.—is diminished. Schools and institutions become poorer, whereupon the people with the resources leave, lessening the ability to develop new resources. To have sustainable communities requires human capacity development. Historically, that was done by parents and the community.

A Model That Can Be Used to Impact Two Generations at Once

The continuum (link to continuum http://ahaprocess.com/files/Bridges_Continuum.pdf) was created for communities involved in developing human capital and community sustainability. The use of the continuum brings all sectors to the decision-making table to build a comprehensive approach for addressing poverty. Our ideas are being applied in numerous communities (including those that are largely African American, Appalachian, Native American, rural, and urban), such as South Bend, IN; Youngstown, OH; Boulder, CO; Battle Creek, MI; Pensacola, FL; and Keshena, WI ... to name a few.

To use the continuum, the columns across the top illustrate these points:

Comprehensive strategies to address poverty and build prosperous communities must stretch from cradle to grave.

Every section of the continuum benefits from the preceding section and can contribute to the success of the following sections. For example, K–12 schools benefit when the parents of preschool children and the early-childhood providers do a good job of brain development. Children come to school ready to learn. In turn, the post-secondary field benefits when K–12 graduates more students who are proficient in math and science and have the skills to compete with students from Asia.

Wellness, high resources, and a balanced, healthy life are the goal. Remember our definition of poverty is "the extent which an individual does without resources." Therefore, the more resources the better.

Community action is needed to help build the good life. Many communities—especially in recent months—are in survival mode themselves and cannot guarantee their citizens a stable, wealth-creating environment ... thus the column for community prosperity. As educators we know how this affects us in the classroom.

The success that one has at work ultimately folds back to provide a benefit to the children of the worker—the children you teach.

Employers benefit too. This includes you, because the retention rate improves and the employees who complete a post-secondary certificate or degree have the skill sets needed by the employer.

The rows illustrate these points:

Metrics: A community must have simple but meaningful measures.

Fallout costs: The community must address poverty from both "heart" and "head." To have one in five U.S. children living in the high-stress environment of poverty is not acceptable from the social justice point of view (the heart). But poverty is too costly in economic terms (the head) too. Thus the fallout costs in terms of outcomes and dollars.

Family of strategies: At aha! Process we offer information that changes mindsets, models that provide structure for change, strategies that cover all causes of poverty, and tools for doing the work. We are developing partnerships with organizations like Move the Mountain, which provides the Circles Initiative with us (www.movethemountain.org). We also have champions in many sectors: schools, business, healthcare, etc., that are learning centers for others in their fields.

Responsibility: To address poverty effectively we must engage the whole community: all classes, all races, all sectors, and all political persuasions. This row gives every organization that encounters people in poverty—or that is responsible for wealth creation or building a prosperous community—a role to play.

Why Would a School Want to Develop Two Generations at Once?

Many schools are now realizing that they cannot educate "in a silo." The children come to school only about one-fourth of the hours in a day. Parents and the community play a huge role in educating the child as well. Since Title I requires parent training, why not play a larger role in the well-being of the community? For many communities, the school is the center of the community. It is only with a critical mass of resourced individuals that communities become more sustainable. Furthermore, the adults are then more active in the development of their own children.

What Does Developing Human Capacity in Parents Mean?

Parent training for parents in poverty includes giving adults language to talk about their own experience, having adults develop their own future story, teaching adults to plan and ask questions, teaching them how to analyze and leverage their own resources, and building their own literacy base by recording their personal stories. It teaches them how to develop and leverage the resources in their communities and how to do it for their children. It builds bridging social capital (Putnam, 2000) in adults, i.e., meeting people who are different from you, which is critical for getting new ideas and building stronger communities.

Community Sustainability and P-20 Involvement

Across the United States we find the development of P-20 initiatives, which are Education Commission for the States and Federal Reserve Board initiatives to integrate the workforce development/ skills with the educational development/skills of all individuals from preschool to age 20. This is part of a larger U.S. economic development push and will closely involve school districts. By using this model, your community can begin your P-20 efforts early, as well as impact the well-being of the community.

Conclusion

We may be weary and feel that our influence is minimal, but it is not. When we are able to keep industry in our home community, when college graduates come back to live and work in our town, when graduation rates are high, and when we have a community where everyone is doing well, then we can know that as educators we've done our piece of supporting the success of the life continuum.

I encourage you to respond to the economic downturn by reviewing this continuum. The future of our schools and communities rests in part on how well we as school people work with all sectors in the community for the success of all. To contact aha! Process for more detail around this document and the sphere of influence you can have on your kids—children who become your community—please call (800) 424-9484.

References

Circles campaign. (n.d.). Retrieved March 18, 2009, from http://www. movethemountain.org/circlescampaign.aspx

DeVol, P. E. (2006). *Getting ahead in a just-gettin'-by world: Building your resources for a better life.* Highlands, TX: aha! Process.

Dounay, J. (2009, January 29). *Improving high school to college transitions: The role of P-20* [PowerPoint presentation]. Retrieved March 18, 2009, from www.ecs.org/html/educationissues/High-School/NEBHEP-20_1-09.ppt

Hart, B., & Risley, T. R. (1995). *Meaningful differences in the everyday experience of young American children.* Baltimore, MD: Paul H. Brookes.

Kishiyama, M. M., Boyce, W. T., Jimenez, A. M., Perry, L. M., & Knight, R. T. (in press). Socioeconomic disparities affect prefrontal function in children. *Journal of Cognitive Neuroscience.* Available from http://www.mitpressjournals.org/doi/abs/10.1162/jocn.2009.21101

Miller, S. (2007). *Until it's gone: Ending poverty in our nation, in our lifetime.* Highlands, TX: aha! Process.

Miller, S., & DeVol, P. E. (2009). Comprehensive strategies for bridges steering committees: The bridges continuum. Retrieved March 18, 2009, from http://ahaprocess.com/files/Bridges_Continuum.pdf

Najman, J. M., Hayatbakhsh, M. R., Heron, M. A., Bor, W., O'Callaghan, M. J., & Williams, G. M. (2008). The impact of episodic and chronic poverty on child cognitive development. *The Journal of Pediatrics, 154*(2), 284–289.

Payne, R. K., DeVol, P. E., & Smith, T. D. (2006). *Bridges out of poverty: Strategies for professionals and communities.* Highlands, TX: aha! Process.

Poor children's brain activity resembles that of stroke victims, EEG shows. (2008, December 6). Retrieved March 18, 2009, from http://www.sciencedaily.com/releases/2008/12/081203092429.htm

Putnam, R. D. (2000). *Bowling alone: The collapse and revival of American community.* New York, NY: Simon & Schuster.

Schamberg, M. (2008). The cost of living in poverty: Long-term effects of allostatic load on working memory. Retrieved March 18, 2009, from http://ecommons.library.cornell.edu/bitstream/1813/10814/1/Schamberg%20-%20Pov%2c%20Load%2c%20Working%20Mem.pdf

Health and Poverty Through the Lens of Economic Class

An Invitation to Healthcare Providers to Create New Models for Better Serving People in Poverty

with Philip E. DeVol

THE UNITED STATES IS NOT DOING WELL in international rankings of quality-of-life indicators. The OECD (Organisation for Economic Co-operation and Development) ranks the U.S. third from the top of 30 nations for the greatest disparity in income ratio between the top and bottom 10% of households, just behind Mexico and Turkey (p. 197, *Measure of America*). The OECD also ranks the U.S. 24th of 24 in Health and Safety indicators. And in the UNICEF Measures of Child Well-Being 2007 REPORT CARD, the U.S. ranked 20th out of 21 countries in child well-being.

The correlation between poverty and ill health is well-established. In his book *Why Zebras Don't Get Ulcers,* Robert Sapolsky describes the socioeconomic status (SES) gradient where there is better health every step up the economic ladder. The wealthier you are, the healthier you are. The corollary also is true. The poorer you are, the sicker you are. Sapolsky finds that the U.S. has the worst SES gradient of the 13 industrialized countries in the study (pp. 301–305). Poverty is associated with increased risk of cardiovascular disease, respiratory disease, ulcers, rheumatoid disorders, psychiatric diseases, and several types of cancer. He says, "For centuries, it's been true that if you want to increase the odds of living a long and healthy life, don't be poor" (p. 300).

Given the disproportionate amount of death and early death in poverty, do individuals have access to the people, strategies, and support systems necessary to address the emotional wounds? Unaddressed emotional issues often lead to physical health issues (Myss, 1996).

In *The Status Syndrome Marmot* (2005) states that the poorer you are, the greater your risk of death. In a panel study of income dynamics, Marmot illustrates the relative risk of death in the United States. His findings are based on data from a study by McDonough (1997) of 8,500 men and women who were followed for 20 years, 1972–91, or until they died. The study shows the risk of dying in relation to average household income in 1993 dollars. Marmot represents the risk of death in each group relative to the best-off group—those with a household income of $70,000 or higher who were arbitrarily assigned a risk of dying of 1, then all other groups were compared with them. Those with household incomes of $50,000 to $70,000 had a risk of 1.34 or 34% more likely to die in the 20-year period. People with incomes of $30,000 to $50,000 had a risk of 1.59, or 59% more likely to die, and so on. For example, those earning $20,000 to $30,000 had a risk of 2.21, whereas households earning $15,000 to $20,000 had a risk of 3.04. Those at the bottom, with a household income of under $15,000, had a risk of 3.89, almost four times the rate of the best-off group. These figures were adjusted for differences in age, sex, race, family size, and period. When the amount of education is taken into account, the impact of income on mortality is reduced.

The process of grieving outlined by Kübler-Ross (1969) indicates there are five stages of grief: denial, anger, bargaining, depression, and acceptance. Who helps with this grieving when language is limited, when another death comes before acceptance comes for the previous death, when depression stays and doesn't leave, and when the support systems are thin with limited access to behavioral health professionals?

Furthermore, brain research indicates that external experience can impact the internal chemicals that are manufactured by the brain for processing of information. In resourced households, death is traumatic. In under-resourced households, death is often an additional unhealed wound.

The purpose of this paper is to identify the complexities found at the intersection of poverty and healthcare using the lens of economic class. Understanding the impact of poverty on individuals and families can lead to a paradigm shift and, ideally, to better outcomes. We are not going to offer solutions but, instead, are going to invite healthcare providers who are attracted to our work to create new models by applying our constructs and tools together with their best practices. The range of potential partners in healthcare is wide. Partners may come from professionals in such health-related areas as prenatal care, infant mortality, immunizations, lead poisoning, dental care, obesity/diabetes, safety/violence, nutrition/diet, addiction, mental illness, and depression. This process has developed new approaches with proven results that improve the lives of people in poverty in other sectors, such as business, criminal justice, education, and community development.

One such champion is Cascade Engineering, a plastics firm in Grand Rapids, Michigan. Fred Keller, the owner and CEO, says, "Our future employees are coming from poverty; we should be good at working with them." To be good at working with someone in poverty, we must understand the impact that poverty has on individuals, families, and communities. This means confronting the myths and misunderstandings about poverty and developing an accurate mental model upon which to build our plans.

In this paper we identify some of the complexities that exist at the intersection of poverty and healthcare that aren't part of the standard lexicon but arise from the findings of *A Framework for Understanding Poverty* (1996, 2005). What follows is not an exhaustive list but enough to illustrate the depth of the work that lies ahead with any healthcare entity that wishes to apply our constructs and use our tools.

Perhaps the best way to present the new information is to stay with Sapolsky who, with Aaron Antonovsky, introduced the concept of social coherence as a barrier to better healthcare for people in poverty. They argue that access—or the lack of access—to healthcare is not the only important variable. According to Antonovsky in *Why Zebras Don't Get Ulcers,* "[T]he poor lack a strong sense of social 'coherence' that contributes significantly to their poor health" (p. 306).

Sapolsky and Antonovsky assert that social coherence can be determined by the answers to the following *five questions.* We'd like to expand on those questions in order to illustrate new insights provided by aha! Process.

"Does a person have a sense of being linked to the mainstream of society, of being in the dominant subculture ...?"

While people in poverty may strive to be part of the mainstream, they find out that they aren't when they encounter the healthcare system. As described in Sapolsky's book, people in poverty are often treated with disrespect or even contempt when they seek help. It's as if they aren't quite American enough to qualify for respectful treatment.

Most of the institutions of the land are run on middle-class rules and norms. Members of the middle class often normalize their societal experience and, assuming that everyone shares their mindset, design programs, policies, and procedures accordingly. Of course, not everyone experiences life in the U.S. the same way; the greater the disparity in income and wealth, the greater the differences in the societal experience. Professionals are familiar with diversity trainings designed to help them better understand their patients from various racial, ethnic, and cultural backgrounds. What they usually lack is an understanding of the impact of poverty and economic class.

In addition, the power that goes along with running and being able to navigate the systems is often invisible to those in the middle class. But people who have little power or influence, who may not have the ability to navigate the systems smoothly (and who might not even have the power to stop bad things from happening to them) are hyper-vigilant about who has power and who doesn't. When individuals with little power are disrespected by those with power, their only option to maintain self-respect is to leave, to separate themselves from the person who has disrespected them. People will tend to avoid institutions where they have been treated badly.

Organizations that have applied aha! Process constructs successfully base their work on relationships of mutual respect. Many healthcare organizations are trying to get their patients and the public to change the way they think and behave when in fact their own thinking and behavior are often bigger issues. To paraphrase Dr. James Comer, a well-known author in the education field, virtually no significant learning or change takes place without a relationship of mutual respect.

"Can a person perceive society's messages as information, rather than as noise? In this regard, the poor education that typically accompanies poverty biases toward the latter."

There's no doubt that healthcare professionals have important health messages for us. But countless healthcare and social work professionals who have attended our seminars have told us that when they are pitching their messages they have seen the eyes of people from poverty glaze over. It's as if the presenter had suddenly been transformed into Charlie Brown's teacher (in "Peanuts"): "Waa waa waa."

This has to do with the registers of language that we learn to use in our homes. The world of work, school, and healthcare operates according to formal register, which calls for specific word choice, a big vocabulary, proper grammar and syntax, and the use of language to negotiate and explore different points of view. Some people in poverty are raised with casual register, which means a relatively small vocabulary and a reliance on reading non-verbals and the social context. People who have only casual register tend to be masters of reading body language and social nuance. Densely written material and lecturing in the formal register turns words into "noise" for those in poverty.

Organizations that have applied aha! Process constructs develop strategies for communicating information that doesn't rely on formal register alone and, when time allows, will teach formal register to their consumers, clients, or patients.

"Has a person been able to develop an ideal set of coping responses for dealing with society's challenges?"

Poverty is a societal challenge. When the price of both gasoline and milk went to four dollars a gallon, many of the working poor were working for just two gallons an hour (Shipler). Poverty today is an unstable, unpredictable, vulnerable environment where you don't know what will break down next. The breakdown of a car leads to a negative chain reaction of events: You're late to work; you can't pick up your kids; and you spend the day solving those three concrete, immediate problems. People in poverty are problem solvers. They use reactive skills to fix problems on the fly. They use their relationships to fix problems. It isn't triple A that helps you with your car, it's Uncle Ray. The more people you have to help you get by, the better.

Poverty, as a societal challenge, isn't just about the choices of the poor. Research shows that there are three other causes: the lack of human and social capital in the community, exploitation of people in poverty, and political/economic structures. These are all societal challenges.

In addition to poverty as a challenge, people in poverty experience other common challenges: disabilities, discrimination, and crime, to name just three.

It's important that we have an accurate mental model of what poverty is like; without it our plans, programs, policies, and procedures will be based on faulty information.

aha! Process has tools to help people in poverty examine the impact of poverty on themselves and their community. Out of this learning experience people often develop new coping strategies and problem-solving skills that allow them to break out of the cycle of dealing with the same concrete problems over and over again. Organizations and communities that use aha! Process constructs also develop ways to provide long-term support for people who are making the transition out of poverty.

"Does a person have the resources to carry out plans?"

Before going to this step we would insert another question: "Does the individual use planning strategies?"

As already noted, people in poverty are problem solvers; but living in an unstable environment requires instant fixes and reactive skills that usually don't involve planning. In poverty, people are afraid for today; they live in the tyranny of the moment with a time horizon of one day to two weeks. A common expression is "I can't see past next week."

By comparison, a middle-class environment is generally stable. Most middle-class people aren't afraid for today because their resources—insurance, money to pay for repairs or childcare, and social connections—help them smooth out rough edges. The stability they enjoy gives them a future orientation that, coupled with a driving force of achievement, makes them natural planners.

Middle-class planners and program designers may have normalized their planning skills, not recognizing that the "tyranny of the moment" is a key feature of life in poverty and that people in poverty may use reactive skills more than planning skills.

Healthcare organizations, on the other hand, base much of their work with clients and patients on the use of plans. It's a tool for moving people through a change process, a way to organize and monitor changes in thinking and behavior. According to informal surveys we conduct during our workshops, healthcare professionals tell us that people in poverty are in contact with three to nine community organizations a year. Every one of those organizations requires a plan.

Organizations and communities that use aha! Process constructs have strategies to help professionals and people in poverty address this problem. It's possible to live in the tyranny of the moment, to be solving concrete problems all day, and still make a choice to move to the abstract in one's thinking and planning.

Returning to Sapolsky/Antonovsky, "Does a person have the resources to carry out plans?"

Framework defines poverty as the extent to which a person does without resources. Those resources include financial, mental, emotional, physical, social, spiritual, role models, and knowledge of the hidden rules of class. Given the unstable world of poverty, a person may start life with fewer resources or may lose resources over time and end up in poverty. Living in the tyranny of the moment and in persistent and concentrated poverty makes it difficult to build resources, but that is exactly what is needed to get out of poverty.

To carry out plans it helps if one has the resources to:

- Purchase the goods and services to stabilize the environment (financial)
- Think in the abstract, to keep oriented to the future, even while being forced to deal with daily concrete problems (mental)
- Use positive self-talk and maintain the determination to stay with the plan even when exhausted (emotional)
- Stay well and have the stamina to keep moving even when beset by depression (physical)
- Get the emotional, physical, and financial support of others while the plan slowly evolves (social)
- Access an inner strength, a high power, and/or a spiritual fellowship that provides motivation and sustaining strength in hard times (spiritual)
- Get help and guidance from a mentor, sponsor, or guide (role models)
- Navigate new experiences and settings with confidence (knowledge of hidden rules of class)

In a society normalized to stability and planning, these things appear automatic. Assuming that others live the same societal experience leads to poor program designs. Organizations and communities that use aha! Process constructs are intentional about building resources.

"Does a person get meaningful feedback from society; do their messages make a difference?"

When we have normalized the middle-class world, we plan for people in poverty; we talk about them, for them, and to them, but not with them. This goes back to our mental model of people in poverty. If we think they are needy, deficient, diseased, and not to be trusted—and base our planning on that mindset—our outcomes will seldom be good. If, on the other hand, we recognize that people in poverty are problem solvers and we engage them in finding solutions, we'll generally get better outcomes. We need to bring people from all classes to the planning and decision-making table.

To their credit, some organizations do include people in poverty on advisory boards and sometimes even on governing boards. We have found, however, that typically people in poverty don't feel comfortable in those settings. And it's no wonder, given that they may not know the hidden rules of the organization or the board room.

The hidden rules of class arise from the environments in which people live; they are about belonging. When people in middle class and poverty have a common language—the lens of economic class—they can use their knowledge of the hidden rules to make relationships of mutual respect and to resolve conflicts. With knowledge of the hidden rules, people in poverty and people in middle class and wealth can more readily come together to solve problems.

Organizations and communities that use aha! Process constructs bring people from all classes, races, sectors, and political persuasions to the table to plan programs and develop strategies. People in poverty have information that is vital to the success of the endeavors, and they can take an active part in doing the work.

Conclusion

We trust that this brief look at social coherence through the lens of economic class hints at the size and complexity of the barriers that healthcare organizations must address if they are going to achieve better outcomes with patients and clients from poverty. Those who have attended our workshops, read our books, and utilized our tools—and now own the constructs themselves—may be in a position to apply our work in new ways.

We recognize that early adapters, not the innovators, are the principal agents of change. aha! Process has the tools to help individuals, organizations, and communities move from theory to practice. We seek to work with organizations that are financially and emotionally healthy and well-led—and where the CEO can get things done and has the full backing of the board. Healthy organizations can shift paradigms more easily than those in distress. Together we would like to achieve proven results that can evolve into high-impact strategies that others can adopt.

Bibliography

Burd-Sharps, S., Lewis, K., & Martins, E. B. (2008). *The measure of America: American human development report, 2008–2009: a joint publication of the Social Science Research Council.* New York, NY: Columbia University Press.

Child poverty in perspective: an overview of child well-being in rich countries (2007). Retrieved November 2007 from www.unicef.org/media/files/ChildPovertyReport.pdf

DeVol, P. E., Payne, R. K., & Dreussi Smith, T. (2006). *Bridges out of poverty: Strategies for professionals and communities* (4th ed.). Highlands, TX: aha! Process.

Kübler-Ross, E. (1969, 1997). *On death and dying.* New York, NY: Simon & Schuster.

Marmot, M. G. (2005). *The status syndrome: How social standing affects our health and longevity.* New York, NY: Henry Holt & Company, LLC, Publishers.

Myss, C. (1996). *Anatomy of the spirit: The seven stages of power and healing.* New York, NY: Three Rivers Press.

Payne, R. K. (1996, 2005). *A framework for understanding poverty* (5th ed.). Highlands, TX: aha! Process.

Payne, R. K. (2008). *Under-resourced learners: 8 strategies to boost student achievement.* Highlands, TX: aha! Process.

Sapolsky, R. M. (1998). *Why zebras don't get ulcers.* New York, NY: W. H. Freeman & Company.

What Information Does *A Framework for Understanding Poverty* Have That Cannot Be Obtained Easily from Other Sources?

Why Do Critics Love to Hate It and Practitioners Love to Use It?

WHAT IS IT THAT MAKES *A Framework for Understanding Poverty* (Payne, 1996, 2005) so widely embraced and used by practitioners? Some critics attribute the popularity to the bias of the readers. But that hardly makes sense because so many educators are the first generation to be college-educated in their families. Many of their parents came from poverty, so the information resonates with them. Therefore, what actually does the work offer that individuals cannot get from other sources?

Most studies of class issues are statistical or descriptive and use one of four frames of reference to identify what causes class. These four frames are:

- Individual choices
- Resources of the community
- Racial/gender exploitation
- Economic/political systems and structures

Most current studies describe poverty as a systemic problem involving racial/gender exploitation. Yes, this is a significant contributor to poverty. Such a *sole* approach, however, does not answer this question: If the system is to blame, why do some people make it out and others never do? Thirty percent of Americans born in the bottom quintile make it out of that quintile (Isaacs, Sawhill, & Haskins, n.d.). And furthermore, why is it that the first waves of political refugees who have come to United States in abject poverty usually have re-created, within one generation, the asset base they left behind? They make it out because of human capital. Ignorance is just as oppressive as any systemic barrier. Human capital is developed through education, employment, the intergenerational transfer of knowledge, and social bridging capital. Money makes human capital development easier, but money *alone* does not develop human capital. Furthermore, any system in the world will oppress you if you are uneducated and unemployed.

This analysis of class is a *cognitive approach* based upon a 32-year longitudinal study of living next to and in a poverty neighborhood of mostly whites. It examines the *thinking* that comes from the "situated learning" environment of generational poverty (Lave & Wenger, 1991). It is the accumulation of years of living with and next to this situated learning environment. The book does not assign *moral value* to the thinking or the behaviors but rather says, *These are patterns that you see. These are why individuals use these patterns, and here is what you can do to help those individuals make the transition to the "decontextualized" environment of formal schooling, if they so desire to make that transition.*

In the book *Change or Die,* Deutschman (2007) says that for people to change, three things must happen. They must relate, reframe, and repeat. And that is precisely what the *Framework* book does: It identifies what one must to do develop relationships, what must be reframed to go from poverty to the decontextualized world of formal schooling, and the skills and behaviors that must be repeated in order to do that. And whether one likes it or not, both schools and social agencies have as their bottom line: *change.* That is what they are getting paid to do.

Again, not everyone wants to change. The question is this: Do you have a choice not to live in poverty? If you are not educated or employed, then choice has been taken from you.

So what is it about the book that is so important to practitioners? Why do so many practitioners love to use it?

1. A language to talk about the experience of generational poverty

In order to reframe anything, one must have language to do that. You must have language to talk about your current experience and the experience to which you are moving. Class, just like race, is experienced at a very personal level first and impacts thinking (Lave & Wenger, 1991). The book explains the patterns in the situated learning environment of generational poverty and is very careful to say that not everyone will have those patterns. As one person who grew up in extreme poverty said to me, "Growing up in poverty is like growing up in a foreign country. No one explains to you what you do know, what you do not know, or what you could know."

2. The resource base of themselves or other individuals used to negotiate an environment in order to know which interventions to use

Many professionals think poverty and wealth are related to money. They actually are much more related to a set of resources to which one has access. Interventions work because the resources are there to make them work. If that basic concept is not understood, then any intervention will not be successful. For example, if a parent cannot read (mental resource), then there is no success in asking the parent to read to the child.

3. The basic patterns in the mindset differences between classes so that one can have social bridging capital

In order to relate to someone different than you, there must be enough understanding of that person's reality to have a conversation. The "hidden rules" allow you to understand that there may be different thinking than yours. Members of a group that has the most people (dominant culture), the most money, or the most power tend to believe that their "hidden rules" are the best. In fact, hidden rules are often equated with intelligence. Knowing different sets of hidden rules allows one to negotiate more environments successfully. "Social bridging capital" (Putnam, 2000) are individuals you know who are different than you because they can impact your thinking if there is mutual respect. As we say to audiences, "Social bonding capital helps you get by, social bridging capital helps you get ahead."

4. The key issues in transition

A huge issue for the secondary students and adults with whom we work is transition. If individuals desire to be better educated, make a change in their living situation, end addiction, have better health, or have a better job, then what is it that those individuals need to know in order to do that? We find that they must assess and develop a resource base, develop social bridging relationships, have a language to talk about their own experience and the one they are moving to, and live in a "decontextualized" world of paper/computers. The book provides the understandings and tools to do this.

5. Key issues in the intergenerational transfer of knowledge

Part of human capital is a knowledge base. Knowledge bases are a form of privilege, just as social access and money are. Such knowledge bases also can be passed on intergenerationally. In an Australian study, which followed 8,556 children for 14 years, the researchers found they could predict with reasonable accuracy the verbal reasoning scores of 14-year-olds based on the maternal grandfather's occupation (Najman et al., 2004).

Part of the intergenerational transfer of knowledge is also vocabulary. Hart and Risley (1995) put tape recorders in homes by economic class and recorded the language that children have access to between the ages of 1 and 3. They found that a 3-year-old in a professional household has a larger vocabulary than an adult in a welfare household. In fact, by age 4, children in welfare households had heard 13 million words compared with 45 million words in a professional household. Vocabulary is key in negotiating situations and environments.

6. **The abstract representational skills and procedural planning skills that one has to have in order to go from the situated learning of poverty to the decontextualized environment of formal schooling**

Lave and Wenger (1991) indicate that beginning learning is always about a "situated environment" that has "people, relationships, context, tasks and language." They add that when an individual makes the transition to formal schooling, learning becomes decontextualized. The context is taken away, relationships are not considered in the learning, reasoning is not with stories but with laws and symbols (abstract representational systems). The research indicates that to make the transition between those two environments, one needs relationships and support systems.

Furthermore, in a study released in 2008 using EEG scans with poor and middle-class children, the researchers found that the prefrontal cortex of the brain (executive function) in poor children was undeveloped and resembled the brains of adults who have had strokes. The executive function of the brain handles impulse control, planning, and working memory (Kishiyama, Boyce, Jimenez, Perry, & Knight, in press, p. 1). The researchers went on to state that it is remediable, but there must be direct intervention. So teaching planning is critical for success in the decontextualized environment of school because it is not taught in the environment of generational poverty.

The book provides the tools to assist with this transition.

7. The necessity of relationships of mutual respect in learning

All learning is double-coded—emotionally and cognitively (Greenspan & Benderly, 1997). The nature of the relationship makes a huge difference in how the information is coded emotionally and therefore received. In a study of 910 first-graders, even when the pedagogy of both teachers was excellent, at-risk students would not learn from a teacher if the student perceived the teacher as being "cold and uncaring" (Goleman, 1995).

In short, *Framework* provides the tools to give choice to people who do not want to live in poverty. It provides the tools for practitioners themselves to relate, reframe, and repeat.

Why do so many critics love to hate it?

In the last five years, critics have attacked the work, and almost all are connected with higher education in some manner (adjunct faculty, assistant professors, et al.). A large part of it appears to have to do with the nature of the role.

First of all, researchers ask questions and must have a clean methodology in order to publish. Researchers need to publish in order to get tenure and to keep their job. You cannot publish if your methodology is not clean, your details are not perfect, all the qualifiers are not included, and your definitions are not exact. Researchers are trained to critique ideas, details, theory, methodology, and findings but not to assess the practicality of the suggestions or situations. Furthermore, many researchers believe that "researched" information has much more value than information acquired through "practice." In fact, Bohn (2006) asks, "How had someone so widely hailed in the public schools as an expert on poverty been ignored by national research institutes, higher education, and all the major, published authorities on the subject of poverty?" In other words, the information does not have value because it has not been acknowledged by higher education.

Practitioners, on the other hand, must have solutions to practical problems. Working with people involves a messy social ecology. To keep your job you must handle and solve problems quickly. If you are a teacher in a classroom with 30 students, then details are not the focus, patterns are; methodology is not considered; group well-being ensures safety of individuals; and the focus is on working with each student for high achievement results. Furthermore, there is simply not the time to document all the details or identify the theoretical frames of the situation. Practitioners deal with people and situations and must have a level of understanding about them in order to meet their needs. Change is one of the agendas of practitioners, so efforts focus on that as well.

Why do critics love to hate the work? Quite simply, the work breaks the rules of higher education around the issue of credibility.

1. *It does not document every detail with the source* (Bomer, Dworin, May, & Semingson, 2008).
2. *It does not explain the information with details and qualifiers but rather in patterns or stereotyping* (Bohn, 2006; Bomer et al., 2008; Gorski, 2005).
3. *It does not reference systems issues or exploitation issues or racial or gender information and their roles in poverty. It does not address the macro-level issues* (Bohn, 2006; Bomer et al., 2008; Gorski, 2005).
4. *It does not have a clean methodology. It has a mixed methodology.*
5. *It looks at what students cannot do and what needs to be taught—deficit model* (Bomer et al., 2008; Gorski, 2005).
6. *It can be misused and misunderstood, so therefore it is dangerous* (Bohn, 2006).
7. *The writer self-published. The book is not peer-reviewed.* (It could be argued that selling 1.4 million copies is a form of peer review.)
8. *Race and class are not talked about together. Therefore, the work is racist* (Gorski, 2005). (As an aside, the book does not discuss gender and class together either, and poverty tends to be feminized around the world.)

What seems to be an additional outrage in the criticism is the number of books that have been sold; almost every critic mentions it. Rather than asking why so many people would find the information helpful, the critics belittle the readers as not having enough intelligence to know their own biases (Bohn, 2006; Bomer et al., 2008; Gorski, 2005).

In defense of higher education, however, there is not a good research methodology for social ecologies. Neither quantitative nor qualitative methods address social ecologies very well. Norretranders (1991) explains that the research in entropy leads to the understandings of information technology. Perhaps fractal or chaos theory would provide a better theoretical model for researching social ecologies.

Does it work? Does it help make changes? Does it build human capital?

Unequivocally, yes. In some places more so than other places that use the work. Implementation is always messy and uneven. We have collected research against a set of fidelity instruments for more than seven years in K–12 settings; these data have been compiled by Dr. William Swan and peer-reviewed ("Scientific Research Based Results," 2009).

A few key findings were …

- When using the normal distribution to determine expected frequencies and analyzing the observed versus the expected frequencies: In mathematics, there were twice as many positive findings as would be expected in a normal distribution (statistically significant at the .05 level); in literacy/language arts, there were three times as many positive results as would be expected in a normal distribution (statistically significant at the .001 level).

- These results led Swan to conclude, "The large number of statistically significant findings for the Payne School Model strongly supports the efficacy of the Model in improving

student achievement in mathematics and English/reading/
literacy/language arts."

- Additionally, an external review of nine research reports
on the Payne School Model, led by Dr. C. Thomas Holmes
(n.d.), professor at the University of Georgia, was completed.
Holmes, along with four other reviewers, concluded that
the design employed in these studies was appropriate, the
statistical tests were well-chosen and clearly reported, and
the author's conclusions followed directly from the obtained
results.

We also have hard data about the impact on adults as well. Using
Getting Ahead in a Just-Gettin'-By World by Phil DeVol, using con-
cepts and tools in *Framework*, we are seeing phenomenal results.
YWCA National named "Bridges Out of Poverty/Getting Ahead" as
a model program in December 2008. These are the results that the
YWCA of Saint Joseph County, Indiana, is getting.

Increase in participants:	Positive change in 3 months	Positive change in 6 months
Income	26%	84%
Education	36%	69%
Employment	32%	63%
Support Systems	13%	84%

Conclusion

The book is about developing human capital through relationships
and education at the micro level.

I am baffled why the discussion so often must be polarized; in other
words, if one idea is right, then another idea must be wrong. Poverty is multifaceted. In fact, the subject is analogous to the six blind
men and the elephant. If we are ever going to successfully address
poverty, it will take all the ideas, as well as greater understandings
than we have at present.

References

Bohn, A. (2006). Rethinking schools online: A framework for understanding Ruby Payne. Retrieved April 27, 2009, from www.rethinkingschools.org/archive/21_02/fram212.shtml

Bomer, R., Dworin, J., May, L., & Semingson, P. (2008). Miseducating teachers about the poor: A critical analysis of Ruby Payne's claims about poverty. *Teachers College Record, 110,* 2497–2531.

DeVol, P. E. (2004). *Getting ahead in a just-gettin'-by world: Building your resources for a better life* (2nd ed.). Highlands, TX: aha! Process.

Deutschman, A. (2007). *Change or die: The three keys to change at work and in life.* New York, NY: HarperCollins.

Goleman, D. (1995). *Emotional intelligence: Why it can matter more than IQ.* New York, NY: Bantam Books.

Gorski, P. (2005). *Savage unrealities: Uncovering classism in Ruby Payne's framework* [Abridged version]. Retrieved April 27, 2009, from http://www.edchange.org/publications/Savage_Unrealities_ abridged.pdf

Greenspan, S. I., & Benderly, B. L. (1997). *The growth of the mind and the endangered origins of intelligence.* Reading, MA: Addison-Wesley.

Hart, B., & Risley, T. R. (1995). *Meaningful differences in the everyday experience of young American children.* Baltimore, MD: Paul H. Brookes.

Holmes, C. T. (n.d.). Review of program evaluations. Retrieved April 27, 2009, from http://www.ahaprocess.com/files/R&D_School/ ExternalReviewRevised.pdf

Isaacs, J. B., Sawhill, I. V., & Haskins, R. (n.d.). Getting ahead or losing ground: Economic Mobility in America. Retrieved April 27, 2009, from http://www.pewtrusts.org/uploadedFiles/ wwwpewtrustsorg/Reports/Economic_Mobility/Economic_ Mobility_in_America_Full.pdf

Kishiyama, M. M., Boyce, W. T., Jimenez, A. M., Perry, L.
M., & Knight, R. T. (in press). Socioeconomic disparities
affect prefrontal function in children. *Journal of Cognitive
Neuroscience.* Available from http://www.mitpressjournals.org/
doi/abs/10.1162/jocn.2009.21101

Lave, J., & Wenger, E. (1991). *Situated learning: Legitimate
peripheral participation.* Cambridge, England: Cambridge
University Press.

Najman, J. M., Aird, R., Bor, W., O'Callaghan, M., Williams, G.,
& Shuttlewood, G. (2004). The generational transmission of
socioeconomic inequalities in child cognitive development and
emotional health. *Social Science and Medicine, 58,* 1147–1158.

Norretranders, T. (1991). *The user illusion: Cutting consciousness
down to size.* New York, NY: Penguin.

Payne, R. K. (1996, 2005). *A framework for understanding poverty* (5th
ed.). Highlands, TX: aha! Process.

Putnam, R. D. (2000). *Bowling alone: The collapse and revival of
American community.* New York, NY: Simon & Schuster.

Scientific, research-based results of aha! Process. (2009). Retrieved
April 27, 2009, from http://www.ahaprocess.com/School_
Programs/Research_&_Development/Scientific_Research.html

What Can the Faith Community Do to Address Poverty? It Can Use a Human Capacity Model That Results in the Development of Resources

Prepared for Good Shepherd Episcopal Church,
Corpus Christi, TX: September 13, 2009.

A KEY ISSUE FOR CHURCHES, COMMUNITIES, countries, and the world today is this: *How can we address the needs of the under-resourced without negatively impacting the resourced?* The words of the Apostle Paul in II Corinthians 8:1–15 are pertinent here: *"Our desire is not that others might be relieved while you are hard pressed, but that there might be equality"* (v. 13). What are the resources that must be identified and/or developed? Community sustainability depends on some resolution of this issue.

The continuum from poverty to wealth is the extent to which you have or can access the following nine resources:

FINANCIAL: Having the money to purchase goods and services.

EMOTIONAL: Being able to choose and control emotional responses, particularly to negative situations, without engaging in self-destructive behavior. This is an internal resource and shows itself through stamina, perseverance, and choices.

MENTAL: Having the mental abilities and acquired skills (reading, writing, computing) to deal with daily life.

continued on next page

continued from previous page

SPIRITUAL: Believing in divine purpose and guidance.

PHYSICAL: Having physical health and mobility.

SUPPORT SYSTEMS: Having friends, family, and backup resources available to access in times of need. These are external resources.

RELATIONSHIPS/ROLE MODELS: Having frequent access to adult(s) who are appropriate, who are nurturing, and who do not engage in self-destructive behavior.

KNOWLEDGE OF HIDDEN RULES: Knowing the unspoken cues and habits of a group.

LANGUAGE: Ability to use formal register, which is the language of work and school, in writing with specific word choice.

Note. Ruby K. Payne, adapted and reprinted with permission from *A Framework for Understanding Poverty,* 1996, 2005.

The extent and degree to which you have these resources determines your ability to negotiate an environment—and to take care of yourself and others. For a long time in social policy, poverty and wealth have been defined against only one resource: financial. Money does not build human capacity, and money does not change thinking. The things that change thinking are:

1. Relationships with people different from you (social bridging capital)

2. Emotional personal experiences

3. Education

4. Spiritual awakening, which comes from 1, 2, and 3

5. Employment

What Causes Individuals to Be Under-Resourced?

Therein lies the rub—and the basic debate about poverty. Alice
O'Connor, in her book *Poverty Knowledge,* states that one of the
reasons poverty has been such a difficult problem to solve is that
there is little agreement on the cause or causes of poverty. In the
research, there are four basic causes given for poverty: individual
choices and behavior, absence of community resources, exploitation,
and economic/financial/government systems.

In the early 1800s the prevalent theoretical construct in the United
States was **genetic** determinism, i.e., who you were and what you
could become were determined by what you had inherited. With the
socialist movements in government and the women's movement
came the theoretical construct of **social** determinism, i.e., who you
were and what you could become were determined by systems and
social access. Social determinism also became the underlying theoretical construct for many social justice and multicultural studies. Concomitantly, colonialism largely came to an end throughout
much of the world.

From the 1960s to 1980s in the United States, many systemic, social
barriers were removed through legislation—but not all. Starting in
the 1970s, as the U.S. moved from industrial to knowledge-based
economies, economic well-being increasingly was and is connected
to education, social capital, and knowledge—i.e., human capacity.
We talk about privilege being related to social class, race, or gender,
and it is. Privilege also is heavily linked to the intergenerational
transfer of knowledge. (1)

For the last 30 years in social policy, social determinism has been
the underlying theoretical construct for legislation, and so a huge
amount of blame has been placed on the "system." The "system" is
bad. All organizations and all systems have at their very essence
two things: relationships and information (Wheatley, 1992). The
human body is a system based upon the information (DNA) and
the subsequent relationships (circulatory, muscular, nervous, etc.)
to form the "system" that becomes your body. **All systems are limited by the capacity of the information and relationships
within that system.** In other words, a system is only as strong as

the individuals within the system and is very dependent upon human capacity.

Furthermore, all beginning learning occurs at a personal level in a "situated learning" (Lave & Wenger, 1991) where we find context, relationships, tasks, and language. Human capacity development begins in a "situated learning" environment and depends on the relationships and information within that environment.

Human capacity development (in this message) is also limited in this way: Some individuals will always need to be cared for; their human capacity cannot be developed to the extent that they can be self-sustaining (mental illness, physical illness, handicapping conditions, age, etc.).

The issue for any community is this: What percentage of poverty can you afford? If too many individuals become under-resourced, eventually the resourced leave, and then virtually everyone is under-resourced. An example of this would be the country of Haiti.

What Is Human Capacity?

When individuals have these resources, they then have human capacity as defined by these characteristics:

- The ability to create/enhance their own resource base: to be self-sustaining
- The ability to make choices that promote dignity, well-being, and continued development
- The ability to give back to others
- The tools to negotiate almost any environment to promote self-preservation, personal well-being, and the well-being of others
- The ability to grow spiritually

What Are the Characteristics of a Human Capacity Development Model?

In short, a human capacity development model is an interactive model of one-on-one relationship building, within a co-investigative knowledge experience, that results in the development of additional resources.

- It is a cognitive model that focuses on knowledge, thinking, and understandings. All learning is double-coded: both cognitively and emotionally (Greenspan & Benderly, 1997). The emotional coding comes from the relationship.
- It is a co-investigative, interactive approach that builds one-on-one relationships of mutual respect with individuals who are different from you.
- It assigns a language to talk about the experience.
- It mediates (tells *what, why, how*).
- It relates to and reframes the individual's personal life.
- It provides the tools to move from a sensory, physical understanding to an abstract, representational concept through stories, parables, metaphors, analogies, and drawings.
- It allows for personal choice.
- It always has a future story at an individual level.
- It results in the development of resources.

For example, Habitat for Humanity is a human capacity development model. In the Habitat for Humanity program members of a family are given the ability to have their own home if they help build/rehab it. In the process, they develop one-on-one relationships with people different from themselves, they gain a knowledge base (how houses are built, how to repair/fix household items, how someone different from them thinks, etc.), learn about money, and so forth. It builds human capacity and in the process, develops relationships.

For example, members of a church in East Texas did this: In their larger community, when a child was born to a young woman under the age of 21, someone in the church would call the mother and tell the mother the church had a gift for the baby—and could she bring it over? The woman from the church would talk to the baby and the mother. Then the woman would ask if she could come back the next week to see the baby even though she didn't have a gift this time. The church woman continued to come every week. In a three-year time period, the babies who had had that visitation were significantly superior cognitively to the babies who had not had the intervention, and each young mother had a mentor and friend. Both the mother and her baby had developed human capacity.

What Model Is Being Used in Many Churches?

The current model in many churches focuses on institutional development. Historically, the church has gotten derailed when it focuses more on institutional maintenance and development than human capacity development.

- Focuses on institutional development, maintenance, and activity.
- Assumes most resources are in place; focuses on the development of spiritual resources.
- Places heavy emphasis on "bonding" social capital (people like you) rather than development of "bridging "social capital (people different from you). Some churches actively exclude individuals because of their differences. (2)
- Knowledge is provided to groups by "authorities"; does not proactively build one-on-one interactions. Positions and knowledge are provided in writing, with little human interaction required.
- Language to talk about the spiritual experience is provided.
- Very few tools are offered to move from a sensory, physical understanding to an abstract, representational concept through stories, parables, metaphors, analogies, drawings.
- Integration of the knowledge into one's personal life is haphazard and related to personal choice; not embedded into the institution.
- Asks church members to give resources to the institution. May or may not develop resources in the members.

To participate in most churches nowadays requires a fairly high level of resources and human capacity.

Why Do We Need a Human Capacity Development Model?

Many people believe that the world's first major revolution was the
development of agriculture, when some individuals ceased their no-
madic existence and began to farm in one place. Many also believe
the second major revolution was industrial, when individuals began
using machines to do their work. The next major revolution in the
world may well be the development of sustainability—the ability
to use resources (education, money, water/land/natural resources,
etc.) and still have them for the next generation. To move to sustainability requires a human capacity development model. When
individuals have limited resources, they need to develop them. The
good news, according to the research, is that resources can be developed—at any stage of life. Yet the very nature of resource development is such that most people can't do it on their own. That's why
the expression "Pick yourself up by your own bootstraps" tends to be
a contradiction in terms. The larger community is needed. However,
that community may have limitations of its own. When a society or
a church has a critical mass of individuals in need of resource development it may not be possible for those who are resourced to continue to give indefinitely without depleting their own resource base.
What the resourced individual understands is that as one human
being, he/she cannot make enough resources to maintain everyone.
Again, here is where the community or the larger religious body
enters the picture because the resourced individual necessarily iso-
lates himself/herself from the demands and needs simply for self-
preservation. This dynamic is most common in large cities around
the world where poverty is widespread and often quite visible. As a
result, there is little community sustainability.

Another reason we need a human capacity development model: our
young people. This is the model they have grown up with on the
Internet—an interactive model of one-on-one relationship building
within a co-investigative knowledge experience, e.g., Facebook and
My Space. They will settle for nothing less.

A third reason is this: The primary model for the development of
human capacity has historically been the family. In post-modern
society, for numerous reasons, this form of development occurs less
and less. The institution that makes human capacity development

its mission will be the institution that rules the next century. Right now human capacity development happens primarily through the media, with very mixed reviews. Is that the model that will develop the capacity we need for sustainability?

Where Did We Get the Human Capacity Development Model? Jesus Provided It

Jesus did not go to the religious organizations, government agencies, or corporate sponsors and say, *Give us money and resources.* No, he went to the people themselves and said, *Let me tell you how you personally can have your own salvation.* And second, he instructed his disciples to provide basic resources within relationships: *"Love your neighbor as yourself"* (Mark 12:31).

- It is a cognitive model that focuses on knowledge, thinking, and understandings. All learning is double-coded: both cognitively and emotionally. The emotional coding comes from the relationship.

   "Ask and it shall be given you; seek and you will find; knock and the door will be opened to you" (Luke 11:9).

- It is a co-investigative, interactive approach that builds one-on-one relationships of mutual respect with individuals who are different from you.

   Jesus' 12 disciples could not have been more different—in personality, in occupation, in background. Furthermore, from the lepers to the Samaritan woman at the well (with five husbands) to tax collectors to prostitutes, even to the dead (Lazarus), Jesus interacted and made deep connections with everyone he met.

- It assigns a language to talk about the experience.

   "For God so loved the world that he gave his one and only Son, that whoever believes in him shall not perish but have eternal

life. For God did not send his Son into the world to condemn the world, but to save the world through him" (John 3:16–17).

- It mediates (tells *what, why, how*).

  "I am the way, the truth, and the life. No one comes to the Father except through me" (John 14:6).

- It relates to and reframes the individual's personal life.

  "But the fruit of the spirit is love, joy, peace, patience, kindness, goodness, faithfulness, gentleness and self-control …" (Galatians 5:22–23).

- It provides the tools to move from a sensory, physical understanding to an abstract, representational concept through stories, parables, metaphors, analogies, and drawings.

  Jesus used these tools constantly, often telling parables and other stories: "I am the vine; you are the branches" (analogy, John 15:5), *the parable of the good Samaritan* (Luke 10:25– 37), *the prodigal son* (Luke 15:11–31), etc.

- It allows for personal choice.

  "Your faith has saved you; go in peace" (Luke 7:50).

- It always has a future story at an individual level.

  "But seek first his kingdom and his righteousness, and all these things will be given to you as well" (Matthew 5:33).

- It results in the development of resources.

  "Give to Caesar what is Caesar's, and to God what is God's" (Luke 20:25).

Many people, including church people, have not understood the brilliance of this model. What Jesus understood was that thinking and the subsequent choices, not compliance, are critical in the development of human capacity, love, and discipleship.

Why Do We Need the Resources and Prosperity This Model Develops?

One of the most damaging interpretations among some in the faith community is that prosperity, by definition, is bad. How incorrect. One person's prosperity helps another prosper and, furthermore, serves as a model for what is possible. Why would anyone want to move out of poverty if there were no better models to move to? I will argue that it's better to have food than to starve. It's better to have shelter than to have no protection. It's better to be healthy than to be ill. It's better to have relationships than to be alone. Quite simply, the better resourced a person is, the more the whole community is sustainable. There is greater opportunity for learning and development because you can focus time on that and not constantly on survival.

Often quoted in this context is what Jesus said to the rich young ruler, a man who had asked Jesus about eternal life, noting that he followed all the commandments. Jesus said, *"Sell everything you have and give to the poor ... How hard it is for the rich to enter the kingdom of God! Indeed, it is easier for a camel to go through the eye of a needle than for a rich man to enter the kingdom of God"* (Luke 18:22,24–25). At that time, to be wealthy was thought to ensure one's entry into heaven. This story often gets interpreted as "It's bad to be rich." Jesus was examining where the man's attachment was— to the physical reality or to the spiritual reality. Often in churches, wealth is seen in polarized terms: either/or. If you have wealth and resources, you cannot go to heaven. Jesus doesn't say that. Rather he says it's difficult to experience spiritual growth when you're too comfortable physically.

Furthermore, a basic rule in nature is this: To receive you must give—and vice versa. The ocean ebbs and flows. Plants take in the air and water and give back food. Prosperity allows for the process of giving and receiving. That includes the giving and sharing of information: *"Give, and it will be given to you"* (Luke 6:38).

What Does the Christian Community Have to Offer Individuals from Poverty?

The faith community has a *huge* pool of individuals who have incredible human capacity—knowledge bases, talents, understandings, language, and resources. The faith community has the potential, if the human capacity development model is utilized, to provide the cognitive, spiritual, and emotional tools for individuals in poverty to become resourced. People ask, *Should I give money?* Money gets you past survival (shelter, food, health), but it doesn't change thinking, and it doesn't develop capacity. I recommend that resources be provided when it's about survival, but all of these resources come with a required component of human capacity development. Knowledge bases are lost over generations. You cannot teach what you do not know. The only way you can get that knowledge and language is for it to be taught by someone who knows.

For example: *food.* Many resourced individuals become frustrated in the grocery store when they see individuals with food stamps or electronic cards buying prepared, expensive food. To prepare food from scratch requires the following: electricity, the ability to plan, pots and pans, a knowledge base about preparing food, measurement tools, math and reading skills, time to prepare foods, a working refrigerator, utensils, plates, and recipes. If you've moved three times in the last three months or you are homeless, you don't have most of these basic resources.

Does the Human Capacity Development Model Work to Help Adults Make the Transition Out of Poverty?

Yes, in our work at aha! Process we have been successfully using this model for five years. We find that it takes two to five years for an individual in poverty to successfully build a resource base that is self-sustaining. We call such resource bases Bridges Communities; they're built upon "Getting Ahead" training. This training provides the knowledge bases and social bridging capital relationships for the development of resources. If you wish to know more about it, go to our website: www.ahaprocess.com. The YWCA announced that a Bridges Community was its model women's empowerment program of the year in 2008. In Youngstown, Ohio, 300 adults in poverty went through the Bridges program and, within six months, 58% had gone back to either technical school or community college for more training and development.

Conclusion

The brilliance of the human capacity model is that it develops resources, provides empowerment, and fosters community sustainability. From that development, we have "systems" that are truly responsive to human needs. In Christianity, discipleship is the call to develop capacity in ourselves and in others. In Matthew 25:35–36 Jesus said, *"For I was hungry and you gave me something to eat, I was thirsty and you gave me something to drink, I was a stranger and you invited me in, I needed clothes and you clothed me, I was sick and you looked after me, I was in prison and you came to visit me."* I believe that Jesus meant this, not only at a physical level, but also at a very cognitive level:

- Hungering for information
- Thirsting for knowledge
- Developing social bridging capital (a stranger)
- Providing comfort and support (sick at heart ... emotional well-being)
- Giving belonging and identity (clothing)
- Giving new ideas (no longer imprisoned); for many individuals, the greatest prison they live in is their own mind

Furthermore, in the parable of the talents, Jesus calls us to develop our talents, saying, "For everyone who has will be given more, and he will have an abundance" (Matthew 25:29).

As Jesus developed human and spiritual capacity by going directly to the people, by providing information and relationships, he also developed community and, among his disciples and other followers, planted the seeds of the church. M. Scott Peck says, "In and through community lies the salvation of the world." We can do no less.

Endnotes

The Serendipity Bible for Groups: New International Version, gives these stages of Christian conversion:
1. Indifference (who cares)
2. Atheist (I know there is no God)
3. Agnostic (I don't know if there is a God)
4. Seeker (I'm searching for God)
5. Commitment to ideas (my church's teachings)
6. Commitment to ethics (clean living)
7. Commitment to persons (doing good)
8. Discovery of fellowship and community
9. Growth in truth (understanding my faith)
10. Changes in my world view and life purpose
11. Changes in my relationship with others

(1) Increasingly, research is looking at the intergenerational transfer of knowledge. A study done in Australia, which followed the children of more than 8,500 women (mostly from poverty) from their first clinic visit for pregnancy, again at age 5, and again at age 14 (Najman et al., 2004), found that the child's maternal grandfather's occupational status independently predicted the child's verbal comprehension levels at age 5 and his or her verbal reasoning scores at age 14.

(2) M. Scott Peck in his book *The Different Drum: Community Building and Peace* says there are four stages of spiritual development: amoral, rule/religion-driven, agnostic, and spiritually driven (see humankind as a whole—not dependent on a particular religion). Peck says churches have individuals in them at each one of these stages.

One of the patterns in some churches is to exclude individuals by assigning "morality" to certain behaviors. For example, some churches exclude divorced individuals, gays/lesbians, by appearance, race, ethnicity, social class, etc. To justify the exclusion, often a Bible verse is given. Yet within that same church there are individuals who are honored who are pedophiles, liars, cheats, domestic abusers, gluttons, etc. The key questions are these: How does any human being move along the continuum of spiritual development if you have no access to those who are at different spiritual levels than you are? How can a human being, in his/her limited understanding, assign value to one of God's creations? When does exclusion protect versus isolate? What does exclusion do to the development of community?

The stages of community building generally include (M. Scott Peck. http://communityx-roads.org/about):

Pseudocommunity
An initial state of "being nice." Pseudocommunity is characterized by politeness, conflict avoidance, and denial of individual differences. Let's be honest; most of us can't keep this up for long. Eventually someone is going to speak up, speak out, and the dam breaks.

Chaos
In the stage of chaos, individual differences are aired, and the group tries to overcome them through misguided attempts to heal or to convert. Listening suffers, and emotions and frustration tend to run high. There are only two ways out of chaos: retreat into pseudocommunity (often through organization), or forward, through emptiness.

Emptiness
Emptiness refers to the process of recognizing and releasing the barriers (expectations, prejudices, the need to control) that hold us back from authentic communication with others, from being emotionally available to hear the voices of those around us. This is a period of going within, of searching ourselves and sharing our truths with the group. This process of "dying to self" can make way for something remarkable to emerge.

Community
"In my defenselessness, my safety lies." [The Apostle Paul says in II Corinthians 12:10: *"For when I am weak, then I am strong."*] In this stage, individuals seek to follow the example of Jesus and accept others as they are—and are themselves accepted. Differences are no longer feared or ignored, but rather are celebrated. A deep sense of peace and joy characterizes the group.

Bibliography

DeVol, Philip E. (2006). *Getting ahead in a just-gettin'-by world: Building your resources for a better life.* Highlands, TX: aha! Process.

Greenspan, Stanley, & Benderly, Beryl. (1997). *The growth of the mind and the endangered origins of intelligence.* Reading, MA: Addison-Wesley.

Lave, Jean, & Etienne Wenger. (1991). *Situated learning: legitimate peripheral participation.*Cambridge, England: Cambridge University Press.

Levite, Allan. (1996, December 19). The "ism" that isn't. (Why social determinism cannot mean what it says). Retrieved from http://www.independent.org

Najman, J. M., Aird, R., Bor, W., O'Callaghan, M., Williams, G. M., & Shuttlewood, G. J. (2004). The generational transmission of socioeconomic inequalities in child cognitive development and emotional health. *Social Science & Medicine, 58*(6), 1147–1158.

New international version of the holy Bible. (1978). Grand Rapids, MI: Zondervan.

O'Connnor, Alice. (2001). *Poverty knowledge: Social science, social policy, and the poor in twentieth-century U.S. history.* Princeton, NY: Princeton University Press.

Payne, Ruby K. (1996, 2005). *A framework for understanding poverty* (5th ed.). Highlands, TX: aha! Process.

Peck, M. Scott. (1987). *The different drum: Community making and peace.* New York, NY: Touchstone/Simon & Schuster.

Serendipity Bible for groups: New international version. (1984). Littleton, CO: Serendipity House.

Wheatley, Margaret (1992). *Leadership and the new science.* San Francisco, CA: Berrett-Koehler Publishers.

Appendix

Lowndes County Schools West Lowndes Elementary and West Lowndes Middle School Columbus, Mississippi 2006–2011	Mississippi

Lowndes County School District, in Columbus, Mississippi, serves approximately 5,400 students, grades K–12, in nine schools. West Lowndes Elementary (WLE) serves approximately 200 students. West Lowndes Middle School (WLM) serves approximately 125 students.

WLE and WLM both utilize aha! Process and the philosophies of Ruby Payne to help transform instructional practice through intensive professional development. WLM has been working with aha! Process since 2006. The first year (2006–2007 school year), all teachers were trained on A Framework for Understanding Poverty, Learning Structures, and Meeting Standards & Raising Test Scores. Each year math and English/language arts teachers at WLM have received four days of academic coaching with aha! Process consultants. The coaching sessions included classroom observations, demonstration lessons, and small group meetings with teachers. English/language arts teachers also received training in Tucker Signing Strategies in 2008. Classroom observations at WLM showed high levels of fidelity to the implementation as measured by achieving a score of 50% or higher on the Instructional Framework Scale—Observation.

WLE began working with aha! Process in 2009. Teachers were trained on A Framework for Understanding Poverty and Research-Based Strategies in August 2009. Teachers at WLE received four days of academic coaching in both 2009–2010 and 2010–2011. The academic coaching sessions have included classroom observations and small group meetings with teachers.

Moving forward, both WLM and WLE will continue to utilize aha! Process to provide intensive professional development through academic coaching and other professional development trainings.

West Lowndes Elementary Results

Achievement gains over time in language arts

In the two years that WLE has been working with aha! Process, third-, fourth-, and fifth-grade students have seen increases in language arts achievement on the Mississippi Curriculum Test, Second Edition (MCT2). The percentage of third-grade students scoring Proficient or Advanced has increased a total of 26.1%. Fourth grade has increased 35.7%, and fifth grade has increased 3.6%.

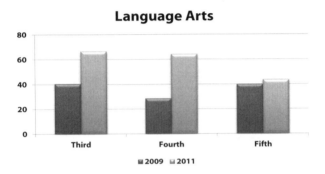

Elementary students demonstrate gains in mathematics over time

Third-, fourth-, and fifth-grade students at WLE have realized increases of 31.5% in third grade, 40.7% in fourth grade, and 16.6% in fifth grade when comparing annual high-stakes test results as measured by the MCT2. Fifty percent of third-grade students scored Proficient or Advanced in 2009, compared with 81.5% in 2011. Similarly, fourth-grade students scoring Proficient or Advanced increased from 34.3% to 75%, and fifth-grade students increased from 47.5% to 64.1%.

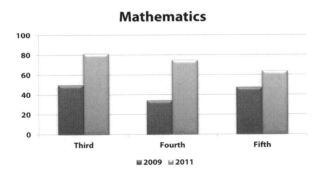

Third-grade students outperform control group in language arts

The percentage of third-grade students scoring Proficient or Advanced on the MCT2 at WLE in 2011 was 36.4% higher than a control group in literacy. In the three-year period from 2009–2011, there was a 26.1% increase in third-grade students scoring Proficient or Advanced at WLE. In the same timeframe, there was a 2.4% decrease in the control group.

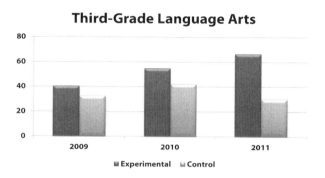

Fourth-grade students outperform control group in mathematics

The percentage of fourth-grade students scoring Proficient or Advanced on the MCT2 at WLE in 2011 was 36% higher than a control group in mathematics. In the three-year period from 2009–2011, there was a 40.7% increase in fourth-grade students scoring Proficient or Advanced at WLE, compared with a 5.7% increase in the control group during the same timeframe.

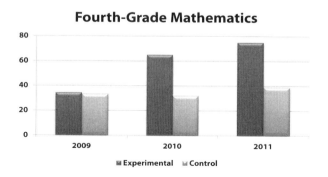

Economically disadvantaged students display academic gains over time in math

Economically disadvantaged students in seventh grade increased performance in mathematics over the six-year period from 2006–2011. Seventh-grade students scoring Proficient or Advanced increased 39% (23% to 62%).

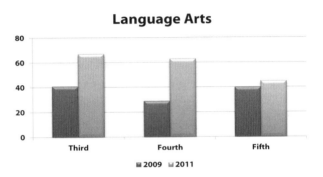

Economically disadvantaged students display academic gains over time in language arts

Economically disadvantaged students in seventh grade increased performance in language arts over the four-year period from 2008–2011. Seventh-grade students scoring Proficient or Advanced increased 11% (30% to 41%).

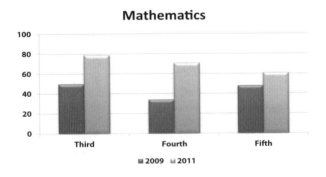

West Lowndes Middle School Results

Seventh-grade students demonstrate gains in language arts over time

Over a four-year period from 2008–2011, seventh-grade students at WLM achieved a 14.4% increase in MCT2 scores. In 2008, 31.1% of seventh-grade students scored Proficient or Advanced on the MCT2. In 2011, 45% of seventh-grade students scored Proficient or Advanced.

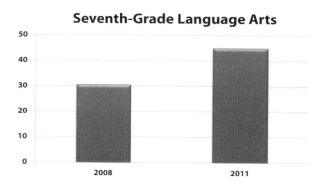

Seventh-grade students demonstrate gains in mathematics over time

Over a seven-year period from 2005–2011, seventh-grade students at WLM achieved a 34.9% increase in MCT2 scores. In 2005, 27.6% of seventh-grade students scored Proficient or Advanced on the MCT2. In 2011, 62.5% of seventh-grade students scored Proficient or Advanced.

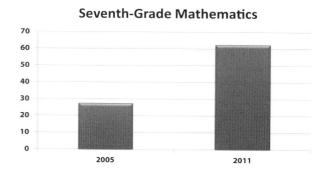

West Lowndes Middle School students outperform control group in language arts

WLM students outperformed the control group in all three grade levels for language arts. The percentage of sixth-grade students scoring Proficient or Advanced was 7.5% higher than the control group. In seventh grade, 24.6% more students scored Proficient or Advanced, and 6.7% more eighth-grade students scored Proficient or Advanced.

2011 Language Arts

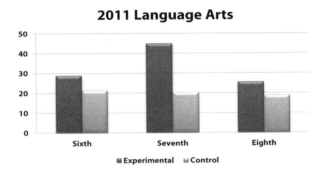

West Lowndes Middle School students outperform control group in math

WLM students outperformed the control group in all three grade levels for math. The percentage of sixth-grade students scoring Proficient or Advanced was 7.4% higher than the control group. In seventh grade, 36% more students scored Proficient or Advanced, and 35% more eighth-grade students scored Proficient or Advanced.

2011 Mathematics

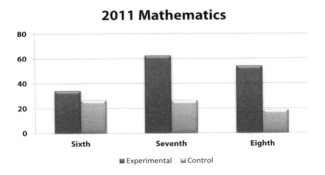

Report Findings—West Lowndes Elementary School

Using aha! Process's Advance: School Improvement, West Lowndes Elementary School students increased achievement over time and outperformed a control group in literacy and math.

WLE students have demonstrated language arts and mathematics gains over time. Data illustrated in this report show that third-grade students realized gains of 26.1% in language arts and 31.5% in math from 2008–2011. WLE fourth-grade students realized gains of 35.7% and 40.7%, respectively, in language arts and math, while fifth-grade students realized gains of 3.6% in language arts and 16.6% in math during the 2008–2011 timeframe.

Furthermore, these students outperformed control group students at a school with similar demographics. Third-graders outperformed their control group counterparts by 36.4% and 25.7%, respectively, in language arts and math, while fourth-graders outperformed the control group by 32.6% in language arts and 36% in math. Fifth-graders outperformed the control group by 18.6% in language arts and 30.7% in math, according to the 2011 test scores reported for the MCT2.

Report Findings — West Lowndes Middle School

Using aha! Process's Advance: School Improvement, West Lowndes Middle School students increased achievement over time and outperformed a control group in literacy and math.

WLM seventh-grade students have demonstrated language arts and mathematics gains over time. Data illustrated in this report show that seventh-grade students realized gains of 14.4% in language arts and 34.9% in math from 2006–2011.

Although there has been greater fluctuation in both sixth- and eighth-grade scores, at all three grade levels students at WLM outperformed control group students at a school with similar demographics. Sixth-graders outperformed their control group counterparts by 7.5% and 7.4%, respectively, in language arts and math, while seventh-graders outperformed the control group by 24.6% in language arts and 36% in math. Eighth-graders outperformed the control group by 6.7% in language arts and 35% in math, according to the 2011 test scores reported for the MCT2.

Research Profile

School Profile—WLE	207 Students, Grades K–5 82% Free/Reduced Lunch 3% White 97% African American 0% Hispanic 0% Asian American 0% Native American
School Profile—WLM	123 Students, Grades 6–8 79% Free/Reduced Lunch 1% White 98% African American 0% Hispanic 2% Asian American 0% Native American
Research Instruments	State Test Data—Mississippi Curriculum Test, Second Edition (MCT2) Implementation Report Data Testimonials
Timeframe	2006–2011

Selected Testimonials

"We are working very hard to implement aha! Process in Lowndes County Schools. We have a very dedicated and committed staff who are working hard to help our students achieve success."

—Dr. Peggy Rogers, Assistant Superintendent, Support Services
Lowndes County School District

"West Lowndes Middle School students and staff experienced reward-ing success and academic growth while working with aha! Process. Our school showed academic growth and met the Adequate Yearly Progress (AYP) goal. The data speaks!"

—Cynthia McMath, Principal, West Lowndes Middle School

Supporting Evidence

DataSpeaks issue 17—West Lowndes Middle School, 2010: http://www.ahaprocess.com/files/ResearchResults_School/DataSpeaks17.pdf

Ridgeroad Middle Charter School
North Little Rock, Arkansas
2006–2010

Arkansas

Ridgeroad Middle Charter School (RRMCS) presented its original charter in November 2002 and was approved by the state in February 2003. RRMCS currently serves 455 students in grades 7–8, 90% of whom receive free/reduced lunch.

RRMCS utilizes aha! Process and the philosophies of Dr. Ruby Payne to help transform instructional practice through intensive professional development. RRMCS has partnered with aha! Process (focused on the principles of Ruby Payne) since its inception in 2003–2004 and continues to have a strong commitment to the processes of this work, as evidenced by the continued planned partnership with aha! Process outlined in its 2009–2010 charter renewal application. Over the years of the charter, aha! Process training and technical assistance have decreased, but the model has been sustained as the teachers have adopted the strategies and implemented them in their classrooms.

At the onset of the implementation, all teachers were trained in Ruby Payne's A Framework for Understanding Poverty, Learning Structures, and Meeting Standards & Raising Test Scores. Training was also provided on middle school concepts. Following these sessions, technical assistance sessions were provided. In addition, 14 days of leadership training and support were provided.

Over the first three years (2003–2004, 2004–2005, and 2005–2006), eight days of technical assistance were provided per subject area in English/language arts, math, science, and social studies per year. (Note: In 2004–2005 math technical assistance was seven days instead of eight.) Non-core subject area teachers received four days of technical assistance in the first year.

Dr. William W. Swan conducted extensive analyses on the impact of aha! Process on RRMCS from 2003–2006. His findings indicate a significant increase in literacy achievement in 2003–2004, a positive impact on literacy and math achievement in 2004–2005, and a significant increase in student achievement in literacy and math compared with traditional approaches in 2005–2006.

Following Dr. Swan's analyses, technical assistance decreased as the strategies became embedded in instructional practice in the classrooms. From 2006–2010 each subject area received a minimum of two days of technical support and a maximum of five days of technical support, typically averaging three days of support per subject each year. Model fidelity continued to be assessed through 2008 as measured by the Instructional Framework Scale – Observation and consistently indicated high fidelity, achieving a score of 50% or higher.

Moving forward, RRMCS will utilize aha! Process to provide intensive professional development in the areas of curriculum development, reading strategies, writing strategies, classroom management, and differentiated instruction to develop literacy in social studies. Emphasis will also be placed to target the academic achievement of the African American male population and special education. In addition aha! Process will support leadership training on the processes of the School Improvement Model for low-performing schools. aha! Process consultants will train building administration and support teachers in monitoring implementation of these processes.

aha! Process/Ruby Payne's Principles

Principle	Ridgeroad Story
Finances do not have to define a student.	Despite the fact that 90% of the students at RRMCS receive free/reduced lunch, students are experiencing success as a result of the aha! Process strategies and core beliefs that are central to the mission and charter of this school.
Relationships are fundamental for student success.	Student relationships with teachers have been improved as teacher mobility has been reduced dramatically, providing students with consistency and reliability from the teaching faculty at RRMCS.
Students need hope/future story.	As students experience continued academic success, they begin to see the world with new possibilities for themselves. This change in belief will guide the students of RRMCS to future achievements beyond their success in middle school.

Ridgeroad Program Results

Achievement gains over time in literacy by seventh- and eighth-grade students

Seventh- and eighth-grade students at RRMCS realized increases of 8% and 5%, respectively, in literacy from 2007–2009 when comparing annual high-stakes test results as measured by the Augmented Benchmark Exam (ABE).

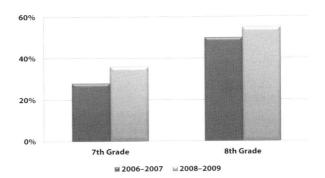

Seventh- and eighth-grade students demonstrate gains in mathematics over time

Seventh- and eighth-grade students at RRMCS realized increases of 14% and 13%, respectively, in mathematics from 2007–2009 when comparing annual high-stakes test results as measured by the ABE. Twenty-eight percent of seventh-grade students scored Proficient or Advanced on the ABE in 2007, compared with 42% in 2009. Similarly, eighth-grade students scoring Proficient or Advanced increased from 30% to 43% in the same time period.

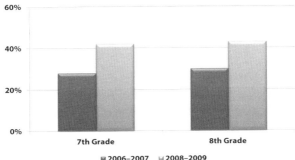

Ridgeroad seventh-grade students outperform control group in literacy and math

The percentage of seventh-grade students scoring Proficient or Advanced on the ABE at RRMCS was 7% higher than the control group in mathematics and 14% higher than the control group in literacy.

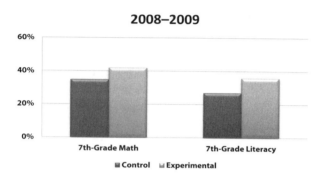

Eighth-grade students at Ridgeroad outperform control group in literacy and math

The percentage of eighth-grade students at RRMCS scoring Proficient or Advanced was 17% higher in literacy and 9% higher in math than a control group when comparing annual high-stakes test results as measured by the 2008–2009 ABE.

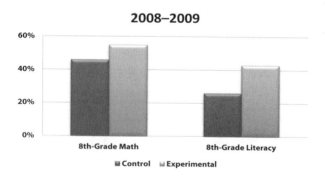

Economically disadvantaged students display academic gains in math over time

Economically disadvantaged students steadily increase performance in mathematics over time, increasing 28.5%, from 21.4% in 2005–2006 to 49.9% in 2008–2009.

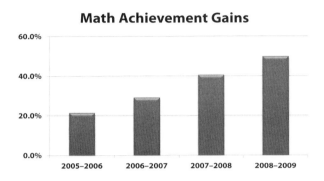

Economically disadvantaged students display literacy gains over time

Economically disadvantaged students steadily increase performance in literacy over time, increasing 15.5%, from 27.4% in 2005–2006 to 42.9% in 2008–2009.

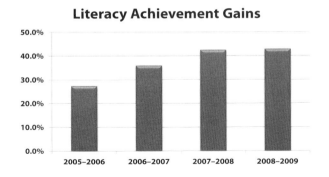

Teacher mobility decreased as a result of aha! Process strategies

Successful implementation of the aha! Process model has decreased staff mobility at RRMCS from 40% in 2003–2004 to 10% in 2007–2008.

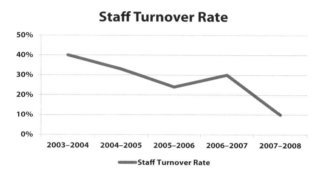

Report Findings

Using aha! Process elements as their foundation, RRMCS has increased achievement over time and is outperforming a control group in literacy and math.

Seventh- and eighth-grade students at RRMCS have demonstrated literacy and mathematics gains over time. Data illustrated in this report find that seventh-grade students realized gains of 8% in literacy and 14% in math between 2005–2006 and 2008–2009. RRMCS eighth-graders realized gains of 5% and 13%, respectively, in literacy and math during the same time span.

Furthermore, these students outperformed control group students at a school with similar demographics. Seventh-graders outperformed their control group counterparts by 7% and 14%, respectively, in literacy and math, while eighth-graders outperformed the control group by 17% in literacy and 9% in math, according to the 2008–2009 test scores reported for the ABE.

When looking collectively at the seventh- and eighth-grade students eligible for free/reduced lunch, these students show consistent gains over time, increasing achievement in literacy by 15.5% and in mathematics by 28.5%, according to a comparison of 2005–2006 test results with those reported in 2008–2009.

Finally, an impact on overall school climate can be seen in the reduction of teacher turnover from 40% in 2003–2004 to 10% in 2007–2008. Teacher mobility was cited by RRMCS as a barrier to student success. As a result of the partnership between RRMCS and aha! Process, this barrier has been dramatically reduced.

Research Profile

School Profile	455 Students, Grades 7–8
	90% Free/Reduced Lunch
	9% White
	82% African American
	8% Hispanic
	0% Asian American
	0% Native American
	5% Limited English Proficient
	14% Special Education
	9% Gifted/Talented
Research Instruments	State Test Data—ABE
	Implementation Report Data
	Testimonials
Timeframe	2006–2010

Validity Review

An external review was conducted through the University of Georgia, led by C. Thomas Holmes, to validate the results of the RRMCS findings from the 2003–2004, 2004–2005, and 2005–2006 school year reports by Dr. William W. Swan. This review revealed the following findings:

- The quasi-experimental pre-test/post-test design with analysis of covariance is an appropriate and sound design.
- The numerical results are well summarized with attention to sample size, adjusted means, direction of difference, statistical outcomes, and probability levels associated with the calculated statistics.
- The reports were controlled for previous years' performance.
- There was assessment for model fidelity.
- Dr. William W. Swan's conclusions followed directly from the obtained results.

Building on this powerful foundation, RRMCS has continued to implement aha! Process strategies with high fidelity. Data indicate that aha! Process strategies continue to have a positive impact on the student achievement of economically disadvantaged students, as evidenced by scores on the ABE in literacy and math, as well as on school climate, as evidenced by the reduction of teacher turnover.

Selected Testimonials

"Time, patience, consistency with strategies, the structure of our school day, and our continuous working relationship with aha! Process have taken us to higher heights."

—Lenisha Broadway, Former Principal, RRMCS

"The School Improvement Model has affected achievement here ... Every year I've had students that have improved in literacy. Last year, out of 110 of my students, 75 of them improved their scores. I've had students who were scoring below Basic and moved up to Proficient, and that's a large gain. And I feel it's because of the strategies that we use and the building of the relationships that we've used through Dr. Payne's philosophies."

—Arclista Story, RRMCS Language Arts Teacher

Supporting Evidence

2003–2004 Report by Dr. William W. Swan: http://www.ahaprocess.com/files/ResearchResults_School/Report_Arkansas_2003-2004.pdf

2004–2005 Report by Dr. William W. Swan: http://www.ahaprocess.com/files/ResearchResults_School/Report_Arkansas_2004-2005.pdf

2005–2006 Report by Dr. William W. Swan: http://www.ahaprocess.com/files/ResearchResults_School/Report_Arkansas_2005-2006.pdf

External Review by C. Thomas Holmes: http://www.ahaprocess.com/files/ResearchResults_School/ExternalReviewRevised.pdf

DataSpeaks Report #1: http://www.ahaprocess.com/files/ResearchResults_School/DataSpeaks01.pdf

DataSpeaks Report #14: http://www.ahaprocess.com/files/ResearchResults_School/DataSpeaks14.pdf

About the Authors

Ruby K. Payne, Ph.D., is founder of aha! Process and an author, speaker, publisher, and career educator. She is an expert on the mindsets of economic class and on crossing socioeconomic lines in education and work. Recognized internationally for her foundational book, *A Framework for Understanding Poverty,* Dr. Payne has helped students and adults of all economic backgrounds achieve academic, professional, and personal success.

Dr. Payne's expertise stems from more than 30 years of experience in public schools. Dr. Payne has traveled extensively and has presented her work throughout North America and in Europe, Australia, China, India, and Trinidad-Tobago.

Dr. Payne has written or co-authored more than a dozen books. With Philip E. DeVol and Terie Dreussi-Smith she co-authored *Bridges Out of Poverty* (1999), which offers strategies for building sustainable communities. Her career-long goal of raising student achievement and overcoming economic class barriers has become the cornerstone of her school-improvement efforts. Sequels to her original *Framework* book (more than 1 million in sales) include *Research-Based Strategies* (2009) and *School Improvement: 9 Systemic Processes to Raise Achievement* (2010), co-authored with Dr. Donna Magee.

In 2011 two of her publications were recognized with awards: *Removing the Mask: How to Identify and Develop Giftedness in Students from Poverty* received a Gold Medal from Independent Publishers for Education, and *Boys in Poverty: Understanding DropOut* (Solution Tree Press) received the Distinguished Achievement Award from Association of Educational Publishers for Professional Development. Both were co-authored with the late Dr. Paul Slocumb.

She received a bachelor's degree from Goshen College, Goshen, IN; a master's degree in English literature from Western Michigan University, Kalamazoo, MI; and her doctorate in educational leadership and policy from Loyola University, Chicago, IL.

 **Philip E. DeVol** has been training and consulting on poverty issues since 1997. He co-authored *Bridges Out of Poverty: Strategies for Professionals and Communities* (1999) with Dr. Ruby K. Payne and Terie Dreussi-Smith, and in 2004 he wrote *Getting Ahead in a Just-Gettin'-By World: Building Your Resources for a Better Life* to help people in poverty investigate the impact of poverty on their communities and themselves.

DeVol works in North America and internationally with communities that apply Bridges constructs, including sites in Canada, Australia, and Slovakia—where Bridges Communities have been awarded two European Union grants to further the work there. Bridges Communities bring people together from all classes, political persuasions, and sectors to address all causes of poverty in a systemic way.

DeVol consults with Bridges Communities on a variety of topics to assist knowledge transfer among the many individuals, organizations, and communities that are adopting Bridges principles in their settings, as well as developing new levels of expertise. In addition to writing and consulting, DeVol works with aha! Process's collaboration with other organizations to implement innovative, high-impact strategies for ending poverty and building sustainable communities where everyone can do well.

DeVol's 2010 book *Investigations into Economic Class in America,* co-authored with Karla M. Krodel, applies the Getting Ahead concepts to college life for under-resourced postsecondary students. This book was honored in 2011 by the Association of Educational Publishers, winning its Distinguished Achievement award for Adult Curriculum (Life Skills); the book was also a 2011 Innovation Award finalist. Finally, a collection of DeVol's essays and articles was published in 2010 under the title *Bridges to Sustainable Communities.*

WE'D LIKE TO HEAR FROM YOU!

Join us on Facebook
www.facebook.com/rubypayne

Respond to our blog
www.ahaprocess.com/blog

Subscribe to our YouTube channel
www.youtube.com/ahaprocess

Download free resources
www.ahaprocess.com

- **Visit our online store for related titles at www.ahaprocess.com/store**

- **Download an eBook**

- **Sign up for a one-hour SHORT COURSE online**